THE OFFICIAL
FORENSIC | FILES
CASEBOOK

THE OFFICIAL
FORENSIC FILES
CASEBOOK

Paul Dowling
with Vince Sherry

ibooks

NEW YORK
www.ibooks.net

DISTRIBUTED BY SIMON & SCHUSTER, INC.

Frontispiece:
3-D animation showing JFK assassin from the
window of the Texas School Book Depository

An Original Publication of ibooks, inc.
Copyright © 2004 by Medstar Television, Inc.
All rights reserved, including the right to reproduce this book
or portions thereof in any form whatsoever.

Distributed by Simon & Schuster, Inc.
1230 Avenue of the Americas, New York NY 10020
ibooks, inc.
24 West 25th Street
New York, NY 10010
The ibooks World Wide Web Site Address is:
http://www.ibooks.net
ISBN: 0-7434-7949-1
First ibooks edition, September 2004

Edited by Judy Gitenstein
Cover photo copyright © Medstar Television, Inc.
Cover design by M. Postawa
Printed in the U.S.A.

Photos courtesy Medstar Television, Inc.
JFK reenactment photos and headshots of Paul Dowling
and of Vince Sherry copyright © Lisa Lake
Photo of Peter Thomas copyright © Gareth Soderquist
of Soderquist Photography
All other photos © Medstar Television, Inc.

Contents

Introduction

People often ask me how I got into this business and how I came to create *Forensic Files*. In 1976, I was working as a summer camp counselor in North Carolina when my mother called, telling me not to return home to Philadelphia because something terrible was happening that no one, not even the world's top scientists, could figure out.

I was following the story in the national press. A large number of convention goers, members of the American Legion, most of whom were staying at the Bellevue Stratford Hotel, were developing a serious form of pneumonia and dying at alarming rates. No one knew whether it was terrorism, a disease process, or even intentional murder.

I returned home, and against my mother's advice, went to the Bellevue Stratford Hotel, and stood outside with other gawkers to watch as investigators searched the hotel for evidence.

It was a fascinating investigation because there were contradictory clues. Most of the dead legionnaires had stayed at the Bellevue Stratford Hotel, but not all of them had. Some of the legionnaires who died never set foot in the hotel, and strangely, none of the hotel employees got sick.

Almost a year later, forensic investigators from the Centers for Disease Control and Prevention discovered the answer. They found a new bacteria, which they named legionella pneumophila, in the pathology tissues from the deceased conventioneers. They theorized it grew in the water pans underneath the air conditioning units on the roof of the hotel. The huge air conditioning fans pulled the water from the pans, which was contaminated with this deadly bacteria, and sprayed it into the air, out onto Broad Street in front of the hotel. That's how it infected some people who never set foot inside the hotel. They were infected just by walking past it. The employees apparently developed an immunity to the bacteria, while the elderly hotel patrons did not.

Reading the CDC's final report, I realized my mother was right all along. I shouldn't have gone down to the hotel. I had been standing right on Broad Street, looking up at the hotel, under the same mist spray from the roof air conditioning units.

Who knows? It may have been my first brush with a real killer.

Reading the report, I first got the idea to do a television series about scientific investigations.

As a teenager, I had a summer job with some of the best storytellers I've ever encountered. No, they weren't journalists, writers, media types, teachers, or anything like that.

They were caddies. Men who made their living carrying golf bags for wealthy country-clubbers outside of Philadelphia. I was a high-school kid doing the same thing, working my way through school. The caddies weren't threatened by us kids treading on their turf. Far from it. They were warm, welcoming, and funny.

They'd bring out their best stories while we waited in the "caddy shack" during rainstorms or until we were assigned the bags we'd carry that day. Some of these guys told stories of their lives and hard times. A few had caddied on the Pro Tour years earlier and would tell us "youngsters" what it was like "looping for the big boys."

Their stories were gripping, simple in design, interesting, engaging, funny, sad, and everything in between. I got a real education in that caddy shack, one I wouldn't trade. It was here that I learned the power of great storytelling.

In the 1970s, my father and I were in an elevator together at Juilliard. I was fortunate enough to be a student there and Dad was in town for a short visit. It was a real thrill when the elevator stopped, the door opened, and in walked the great Mitch Miller. He was a conductor and an arranger who, years earlier, had hosted a very popular musical/variety television series on NBC, *Mitch Miller and the Sing Along Gang.*

Mitch was very cordial, I introduced him to my father, and I told him I was aware he was the producer largely responsible for helping launch Johnny Mathis's recording career for Columbia Records.

Mitch told me an interesting story about that experience. He said Mathis was primarily a jazz singer when he came to Columbia, and he liked to improvise and add other fancy vocal things to the songs while recording. Miller said he told Mathis to "take all of that out," to sing as simply as he could, "so that the listener can say to himself, I could sing that song, too."

That was a lesson I never forgot and as a storyteller, I take Mitch Miller's advice every day. I try to tell stories as simply as

I can, just the way you'd tell the same story to a friend over a sandwich in a coffee shop.

How does that translate to a television show? One day recently, waiting for me on my desk, was the script to one of the *Forensic Files* episodes for my review. By the end of the first page, I was hopelessly lost. I had no idea what was going on or what the crime was about. I called the producer in, put down the script and said, "Tell me the story—just like we're sitting having dinner together." For the next several minutes, he told me a riveting tale of greed and revenge that had me sitting on the edge of my seat.

When he was through, I said, "Okay, rewrite this thing just the way you told it to me."

THAT's storytelling.

The idea for the first *Forensic Files* episode all but fell on my doorstep. In the 1980s, my neighbor was an airline pilot for Eastern Airlines and he had friends visit one weekend from Connecticut: a fellow pilot, Richard Crafts, and his wife Helle, a flight attendant. I only saw them from across the yard but I recall vividly how striking Helle was, a beautiful Norwegian with blond hair.

Several months later, I read a news story that Helle had gone missing and her husband Richard was a suspect in her disappearance and continued to follow the story closely. "The Disappearance of Helle Crafts" was the pilot program for *Forensic Files,* (although the series was called *Medical Detectives* then). It told the fascinating and tragic story of how forensic scientists were able to prove murder without ever finding her body. With just a handful of forensic evidence Richard Crafts was found guilty of killing his wife and putting her body through a woodchipper on the bank of a Connecticut river.

A letter from Richard Crafts turning down our request for an interview still hangs on my wall.

Introduction

Forensic Files (*Medical Detectives*), premiered in April 1996 and I'm happy to say it was an immediate hit. It was the first reality-based true-crime forensic series of its kind and since then has spawned dozens of imitators.

In 2002, *Forensic Files* aired on NBC as a summer replacement. It was the first time in television history that a broadcast network aired a prime-time series originally produced for cable, and it was the fifteenth highest-rated program in the first week it aired.

The series now airs in more than one hundred countries.

People have always loved true-crime stories. But the fascination goes further than that. People are intrigued by these new scientific super-sleuths who can genetically match a seed pod to the tree next to a victim's body. When they find dirt, moss, and pollen in the wheel wells of a car, they can identify its exact location based on the geological evidence. A shard of glass in a suspect's jacket is found to be so different from the broken glass at the murder scene, he was no longer considered a suspect. And the list goes on.

Forensic Files tells the stories of the people who figure all of this out for a living.

My daughter once asked me, as all kids do with their parents, "What do you do at work?"

Searching for some kind of meaningful description, I told her there was a stool with a microphone in front of it and a light bulb hanging down, and every night at the same time I walk out, grab the microphone, sit down and tell a twenty-two-minute murder mystery story about how the police capture the bad guys with science.

Killers always leave something behind. Often invisible to the naked eye, what they leave behind doesn't always look like it would be evidence: a a piece of pollen, a flake of skin, a piece of paper.

The question is, will the crime investigators find it? That's what *Forensic Files* is all about.

I love the show and I love the people I work with. Every Tuesday at 4 A.M., the show's narrator, Peter Thomas, begins his final rehearsal for the script he'll record at precisely 9 A.M. It's one of my greatest pleasures to direct those sessions with Peter because, well, he's simply the best. If you watch the series, you know what I'm talking about.

I couldn't get the show on the air each night if it weren't for Kelly Martin, thanks to her organizational skills, good humor, and patience. I'd also like to thank Vince Sherry for working with me on this book. Vince has been with the show almost from the beginning, and is like a brother to me. I trust his judgment completely. He's one of the smartest and best-read guys I know. I've enjoyed our collaboration—and I hope that you, the readers, will too.

PAUL DOWLING
Allentown, PA
September 2004

ONE
The House That Roared

To the untrained eye it looked like a perfectly normal house. But to homicide investigators it was teeming with evidence, so much so that we called the episode "The House that Roared." The woman who lived there, a forty-three-year old mother of three named Caren Campano, was known for being meticulously neat. As usual, everything in the house was in perfect order—except for one thing. Caren Campano was missing. No one—not friends, not family, not even her new husband, Chris—had heard anything from her. She had been gone for three days.

Chris, fifteen years younger than Caren, was her third husband. Family members weren't optimistic that Caren's third attempt at marriage would work any better than the first two. On the last night she was seen, neighbors heard the couple screaming at each other. The argument was so loud that the neighbors could even tell police what it was about: Caren was insisting that Chris go to rehab to take care of a drug problem that she said was destroying their marriage.

Chris confirmed the fight. He told police that he and Caren

decided to cool off. She went to the store and he walked to a nearby bar. When he returned Caren wasn't there, and some minor items—a television, a stereo, some pieces of jewelry—were missing from the house. Chris thought it was possible Caren had taken the items and was going to live elsewhere until he got help for his drug problem.

But the next day she didn't show up for work and Chris started to worry that it wasn't Caren who had taken the items. He told police that perhaps the house had been robbed, and that whoever did it had done something to Caren.

The story sounded decidedly suspicious to police, especially when Chris's alibi fell apart. No one from the bar remembered seeing him. And he was seen pawning some of Caren's jewelry at a local pawnshop the day after she went missing. The argument heard by neighbors put Caren in the house the last time anyone could account for her whereabouts.

Police theorized that if something had happened to her the house was the place to look. At first glance, everything was spotless. But then, on the bedroom floor investigators saw a brownish stain. It tested positive for blood, and a subsequent DNA test matched it to Caren Campano. But this was hardly proof of foul play. People cut themselves in their houses all the time, and the stain wasn't big enough to indicate a large blood loss.

Nonetheless, this discovery didn't do anything to ease suspicions that Chris Campano had something to do with his wife's disappearance. Police decided it was time to test the entire house. Perhaps, they thought, forensic science could tell them what happened to Caren Campano. They turned to a indispensable tool in the forensic scientist's arsenal: Luminol, a chemical that glows when it comes into contact with the iron component in human blood.

Thousands of killers have tried all sorts of soaps and bleaches to clean up bloody crime scenes, but rarely can they hide from Luminol. Iron is hard to clean, and Luminol almost always finds it. When sprayed on almost any surface that once contained blood—no matter how thorough the cleaning—Luminol will glow.

A glowing bloodstain is a regular sight for homicide investigators, and when they see it, there's both good and bad news. Bad news because it usually means someone has been seriously injured; good news because the blood trail often reveals the responsible party.

Still, Luminol is not without its problems. It will essentially "eat up" the iron in blood, and does it very quickly. This means investigators have very little time—about ninety seconds— to photograph the glowing bloodstains. After that the evidence, and often their case, simply disappears. This glowing is best seen in the dark, so the ideal time for a Luminol test is well after the sun has gone down.

At the Campano house investigators waited for a moonless night, and decided that every surface of the house—both inside and out—would be tested. The chemical dragnet began in the bedroom and investigators were stunned by what they saw.

There was so much blood in the room—invisible to the naked eye, but glowing after the Luminol treatment—that people could actually see each other. It was clear that blood had been everywhere—on the walls, the ceiling, the doors. One veteran police officer later said it was like being "in the middle of a horror movie."

Bloodstains were found throughout the house, and their shapes and sizes told police the story of what happened to Caren Campano. Blood spatter—small, high-impact stains—told them that Caren had been beaten with a blunt object. The density and position of these stains also told them that she had been struck multiple times. The amount of blood indicated she had been struck in the head, a highly vascular area which will bleed profusely after trauma.

A thick swipe of blood on the kitchen door told police that Caren had been carried through the kitchen after this beating; her head had apparently brushed against the door. A large stain in the utility room indicated the killer had put the body there before dragging the body down the backdoor steps. Each of the steps had a distinct bloodstain that glowed in the dark.

But questions still remained. Where was the body? Where was the murder weapon? And was there any proof that Chris Campano had struck the fatal blow? Prosecutors were convinced he was responsible but were up against one of the toughest challenges in law enforcement: a so-called bodiless homicide, which makes it very difficult to get a conviction. Often the mere possibility that someone could be missing is enough to establish reasonable doubt with a jury. In addition, a murder victim's body is always the best source of evidence, and without it a prosecutor is working at a serious disadvantage.

Eight months passed, and numerous searches failed to turn up any sign of Caren Campano. On the strength of the Luminol evidence alone, police were preparing to charge her husband when they got the break they had long been hoping for. A group of young dirt bikers discovered a body. It was badly decomposed but dental records soon provided the identity: it was Caren Campano.

Despite the decomposition the skull was intact, and it told police a story they already knew—the story the Luminol had told them. Caren had been struck multiple times in the head and face with a blunt object.

Chris Campano and his lawyer were called to police headquarters. Investigators said they knew exactly what happened and laid out the whole scenario to their stunned suspect.

"You hit her with a blunt object in the bedroom."

"You dragged her through the kitchen."

"You rested the body in the utility room before you dragged

The Campano's bedroom floor before Luminol. No bloodstains; no signs of cleaning.

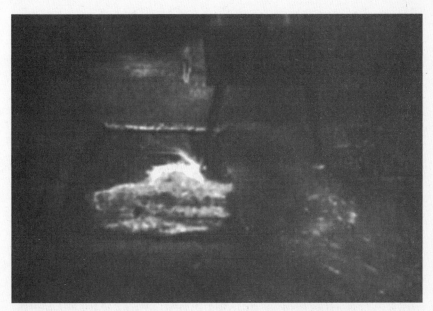

The same floor after the Luminol treatment. Same photo. Same angle. The glowing splotches indicate blood. A detective said it was "like a horror movie."

Chris Campano, who thought he cleaned the crime scene, but Luminol revealed the spots he missed.

her down the steps and into the woods until you could get rid of her."

Realizing police knew exactly what happened, Chris Campano took his lawyer's advice and confessed on the spot. He was found guilty of manslaughter and sentenced to a thousand years in prison. He did everything he could to cover up the murder—and he did a lot—but the Luminol exposed him, and brought justice, if not to Caren Campano, at least to her family.

One of the exhilarating—and unsettling—things about cases like "The House That Roared" is getting intimately involved with every aspect of a murder investigation. Since *Forensic Files* began in 1994, we've produced episodes on nearly two hundred cases. That's two-hundred times we've come to know family members who've experienced unimaginable tragedy; two-hundred times that we've hunkered down with prosecutors and homicide investigators as they took us step-by-step through the process that led them to the killer; and strangest of all, two-hundred times that we've entered the minds of the killers themselves.

Reliving a murder through the eyes of the killer is disturbing, to say the least, but it's the only way to see exactly how the murder was committed. It's the only way to show viewers how forensic science ultimately put these killers behind bars.

Most of the crimes we've dealt with have pitted sophisticated criminals against the forensic scientists whose job it is to reveal their crimes. In the years since *Forensic Files* went into production we have reviewed literally thousands of cases, but, with few exceptions, the only ones we choose—the ones that "make the cut"—are those in which a criminal has gone to considerable lengths to outsmart law enforcement. To highlight just a few of these cases . . .

• A doctor suspected of raping a patient tries to cheat a DNA blood test by implanting a bladder with someone else's blood under his arm. This ruse works repeatedly until investigators take a closer look at the blood . . . and the doctor's arm.

• Two teenagers brutally murder a young woman and spend days burning her body. They then spread the ashes over 300 square miles of northern Michigan. Three years later detectives find just enough to identify the victim.

• A cross-dressing killer leaves the scene of the crime disguised in a dress once worn by his victim. When police find a uniquely shaped bloodstain the killer ends up trading women's clothing for a prison jumpsuit.

It may sound strange, but in cases like these, both sides are trying to tell a story: the killer by manipulating the evidence

19

or trying to hide it, and the scientist by analyzing the same evidence to reveal the actual facts of the case. It's a game of sorts . . . pitting killer against the scientist. But this game is all too real, and the stakes are high. If the killer loses, it's life behind bars, or worse—a one-way trip to death row. If the scientist loses, a smart killer is walking the streets. And as any law enforcement officer will tell you, killers who think their crimes through will almost always kill again.

These are the stories we tell on *Forensic Files*. We try to show how a combination of dogged police work, the occasional bit of luck, and most of all, the incredible arsenal of tools and techniques available to the modern forensic scientist, expose the truth. And after getting intimately involved with so many murder investigations we've found that the tension between killer and scientist can make for compelling television. We've also found that producing these stories can sometimes be a harrowing experience.

Take, for instance, a case we called "Haunting Vision." As in all of our programs, there's a reason for the title. In this case, a woman named Lori Keidel relived an experience from when she was only six years old—she had a vision of a particularly gruesome murder. In her mid-thirties when we met her, Lori had relived the night she saw her father beat her mother to death and bury her body. It was a night where she awoke a few hours later to find her bedroom engulfed in flames.

It was the night Lori's twelve-year-old sister died saving her life.

Her "vision" of this night was so vivid that she was able to provide police with a detailed description of where her mother was buried. So much time had passed that the new owners of Lori's childhood home had built a concrete porch over the spot the body was believed to be. If Lori's story was true, and not some fantasy, the body would be there—but how do you determine if a body is buried beneath concrete? The answer

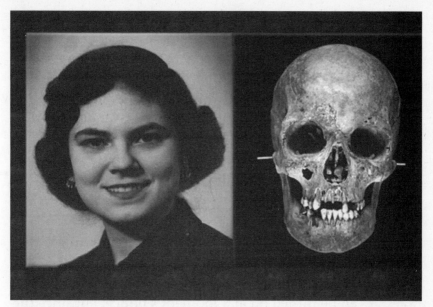

Lori's mother, in death and in life. The skull was recovered exactly where Lori said it would be.

came from an organization with an unlikely name: NecroSearch International. This group of freelance scientists uncovers bodies no one else can seem to find.

By means of a process known as GPR, or Ground Penetrating Radar—a machine that does detailed X-rays of the ground—NecroSearch examined the spot where Lori said she'd seen her father bury her mother thirty years earlier. Many people were skeptical of Lori's "haunting vision," but when the GPR clearly showed a human body buried exactly where she said it would be, her credibility was certified, especially when her mother's corpse, with nylon stockings cinched around what was left of her throat, was finally unearthed. Lori's father was convicted shortly afterward on a charge of first-degree murder.

For us, the only way to show viewers what happened was to re-create the "haunting vision" itself: to show viewers what

Lori saw. It was one of the most demanding, and emotionally draining re-creations we've ever attempted.

First we had to simulate the fire. We hired a group out of New York City that did nothing but manage fires for film companies. If you ever want to film a house burning to the ground, or a car exploding into flames, these are the guys to use. Their response to all of our concerns was a simple "No problem!" For them, setting fires was an everyday affair.

Luckily, one of our producers was kind (or foolhardy) enough to let us use his house. In an upstairs bedroom the "fire guys" as they came to be known, set up three stands of what are known as "fire bars." These are steel rods attached to canisters of propane. Each rod is riddled with holes. The propane is lighted and the resulting flame shoots through the holes. It can be turned off at a moment's notice, but since the flames can reach heights of about six feet, the likelihood of problems was high.

The risk was heightened by the ages of our actresses. In the actual event, Lori was six; her sister was twelve. We needed our actresses to simulate what happened to them. And what happened was among the most tragic stories we've ever heard: Lori screaming when she woke up and found her room in flames, her sister rushing in, throwing her to the ground and covering Lori with her body—the whole time whispering "I love you, I love you, everything will be okay."

But it was not okay. The older sister burned to death, and Lori suffered third-degree burns over 25 percent of her body.

For us, it was a challenge to re-create the event. The director signaled the fire guys to light up the room. Within seconds, sheets of flame were rising from fire bars hidden behind beds and dressers. The room became stiflingly hot. The director yelled "action" and our young actresses—both seasoned veterans out of New York—ran through their paces.

In one scene the camera was low to the ground. The older actress threw her young counterpart to the floor just in front of the lens. She whispered, "I love you, I love you. Everything will be okay," as a wall of flame loomed over them. We watched this on a playback monitor in a separate room, and it was a gut-wrenching experience. What we were seeing was eerily similar to what actually happened some thirty years earlier. Technically, it was "fake" but it seemed real to us. And it was heartbreaking.

The past coming to life is an experience we have with almost every case we film. By the time we re-create a given crime, we are so familiar with the details, and the real-life victims, that the re-creation literally takes on a life of its own.

That attention to detail has produced some unexpected results. For instance, in 1998, the U.S. Justice Department asked us for some copies of our program. When we asked why, they said they wanted to use them for training purposes, which was perhaps the greatest compliment we've ever been paid.

If you've picked up this book you're probably familiar with *Forensic Files*, and may recognize some of the cases. If you're not familiar with the show, perhaps this book will give you some insight into why it has become so popular. So for *Forensic Files* fans and new arrivals, what follows is a brief tour through the unusual place where TV and law enforcement meet—the place where television brings real-life murder investigations to the screen.

TWO
Stranger Than Fiction

People often ask us where we find story ideas. The truth is, our ideas come from a lot of places. We've gotten some from lawyers, others from homicide investigators, some from victim's families, and many the old-fashioned way—by digging through newspapers and the Internet.

Some are almost impossible to believe. In fact, on a couple of occasions we didn't think the stories could be true until we checked them out ourselves. A case in point: In May 2001 we got a call from one our producers. He's based out of St. Petersburg, Florida, and said he had something that was perfect for *Forensic Files*. He then proceeded to tell us about a local man who had just been convicted for the murders of a number of area prostitutes. That didn't sound all that unusual until he told us how the key piece of evidence surfaced: the convicted man's dog was "addicted to nicotine," as he described it, and that's what finally broke the case.

Here's the story, which we called "Treads and Threads."

Clearwater, Florida, is probably known to most people as the place where major-league baseball sets up shop for spring training. But in 1994, shortly after the baseball players decamped to start the regular season, it was the scene of some gruesome violence. Prostitutes were turning up murdered around the downtown area, and it looked to be the work of a seasoned killer. All the victims were found nude and had been sexually violated. Their bodies were always dumped during rainstorms. It was the worst kind of case for homicide detectives: the victims had been chosen at random and the killer had at least some familiarity with law enforcement techniques.

Since the rain had washed away almost all trace evidence from the bodies, detectives had little to work with. But by painstakingly going over the bodies with a Luma-light—a florescent light that makes fibers and other bits of material glow—investigators discovered some tiny pink fibers. Under a microscope the fibers were found to be made of nylon, and they were "tri-lobal" in shape, which meant they were most probably carpet fibers, which are braided. The forensic analyst also found some tiny brown hairs that didn't appear to be human. These were sent to the FBI for analysis.

These hairs are what's known as trace evidence, the "lifeblood" of almost every murder investigation. The term itself tells you almost everything: traces—tiny particles—of evidence are leave behind at crime scenes. Most often trace evidence is hair or fiber but can include almost anything—mud, skin cells (eczema is a serious liability for a murderer), even pieces of dust.

A French medical doctor named Edmond Locard established the principle of trace evidence that now bears his name: the Locard Exchange Principle. Dr. Locard stated that everyone leaves traces of themselves behind when they enter a room, and takes traces with them when they leave. Hence, the "exchange." What this means for homicide investigators is that murderers—no matter how hard they try not to—almost always leave some trace of themselves at the crime scene.

In this case, the trace evidence—the hairs and fibers found on the bodies of the murdered prostitutes—was all police had to work with. They feared they had a serial killer on their hands, and their fears were soon confirmed. A few days later another body was discovered. The details were gruesomely familiar: the victim was a prostitute found naked in the rain. Closer examination revealed the same pink tri-lobal fibers. But this time there was something else. Stuck to the victim's skin, analysts discovered a speck of what was later found to be cigarette paper.

The only other evidence at the scene was a faint tire print found in the sand near the body. Detectives photographed the print and sent it to one of the country's most respected forensic specialists, Peter McDonald. A former tire designer, McDonald now was able to turn his exhaustive knowledge of tires to crime-solving. He took one look at the photo and identified the print. It was from a nearly-new Firestone ATX tire, and judging by the depth of the impression in the sand, he thought it was probably mounted on a small pickup truck.

This was not a popular tire, and when investigators contacted all the dealerships in the area they found only one who sold the model. In the last year they had sold four.

With the addresses of the four buyers in hand, police did a little surveillance work and found that only one, James Randall, drove a small pickup. James Randall had a prior conviction in Massachusetts—for sexual assault. He lived with a woman, Terry Jo Howard, who had at one time been a prostitute.

They staked out the couple's house, and found that every day Terry Jo took a small dog for a walk. Detectives photographed the dog; it was then identified as a pug, a show breed known for its pushed-in face. It was time to call the FBI. Had they identified the hairs that were found with the tri-lobal fibers? Yes, they had. They were from a dog—a pug, to be exact.

This seemed to be more than coincidence to detectives.

James Randall had a history of violence against women, he drove a vehicle that had the same model of tire found at one of the crime scenes, and he just happened to own a pug—the same breed of dog whose hairs had been found on one of the victims. This was good evidence, but it was all circumstantial. Investigators were becoming convinced Randall was a serial killer and wanted something conclusive to tie him to the victims. So they hatched an unusual plan.

Two female detectives were to go undercover as owners of a newly formed dog- grooming company. While James Randall was at work, they went to the house, and told Terry Jo they were offering free dog-grooming services in an effort to generate business. Terry Jo readily accepted and while the detectives were washing the pug they noticed a pink nylon carpet on the floor. On the carpet were tiny specks of paper. They asked Terry Jo what they were, and were told they were bits of cigarette paper. She told the detectives/dog groomers that her pug, whose name was Princess Penny Pickles, was "addicted" to cigarettes. Terry Jo said that every time she snuffed out a cigarette Princess Penny would run over to the ashtray and tear the butt apart so she could eat the nicotine-soaked bits of tobacco that hadn't been smoked.

This, needless to say, was of considerable interest to the undercover detectives. While Terry Jo was in another room they took a piece of the pink, nylon carpet, and also one of Terry Jo's discarded cigarette butts. Once back in the lab, the fibers were found to be microscopically consistent with the fibers found on the victims.

What clinched the case was the cigarette butt. It contained minute amounts of saliva—and saliva contains DNA. The DNA extracted from the cigarette butt was tested against DNA found in the speck of cigarette paper recovered from one of the victims. And it matched. This was what police were looking for, and they moved in to make their arrest.

The DNA from the cigarette paper was compared to James Randall's and did not match—he wasn't a smoker. But it was a perfect match to Terry Jo's DNA, and this was bad news for Randall. It tied someone in his house to the victims, and since they'd all been sexually violated, it clearly wasn't Terry Jo. Randall was eventually convicted of four counts of first-degree murder—all thanks to a pooch with a penchant for tobacco.

This was the kind of story you simply couldn't make up. And re-creating it was no small feat. First, we had to get a trained pug, and second, we had to find a way to get him to tear apart discarded cigarette butts—or at least what appeared to be cigarette butts. The problem was finally solved by one of the creative minds in our prop department. He made a mock-up of some fake cigarette butts and laced the inside of the paper with a liver puree. The dog couldn't get enough of it, and at every opportunity made a beeline for the fake cigarettes. It looked great on camera. As our prop guy watched it he said, "I never thought four years of art school would come in so handy."

When this story broke, a lot of television news magazine programs were interested in covering it. We were fortunate that Terry Jo Howard happened to be a fan of *Forensic Files*. We are the only program she agreed to interview for, and the story she told us was extremely disturbing. Since much of it had to do with Randall's unusual tastes in sex we couldn't put much of it on television, but we can at least share some of it here. Terry Jo was down on her luck when she met James Randall. He had a stable job and appeared to be ready to make a commitment, which was something Terry Jo desperately needed. But this chance at domestic stability was not without a cost of its own.

Terry Jo soon found out that Randall's sexual preferences tended toward violence. During sex he would often wrap his fingers around her throat and simulate strangling her. When she complained, he assured her that she was not in danger—

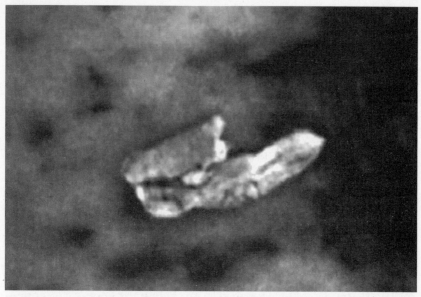

Evidence photo of the cigarette paper found on victim. This tiny speck of evidence revealed a killer.

Princess Penny Pickles, the dog that brought a serial sex killer to justice. Neither she nor her owner knew her passion for tobacco would put him behind bars.

that it was just "fun and games." Terry Jo was once in the business of serving men's sexual needs and was willing to tolerate some unusual sexual practices for some stability in her home life.

But she was scared, and became more so after one incident in which Randall's sex play almost left her unconscious. With her rising apprehension, their relationship began to deteriorate. Terry Jo was thinking about leaving when Randall was arrested for strangling and murdering four area prostitutes. He later told her that he had to kill them "to keep from killing" her. This was a defining moment for Terry Jo, one in which she realized that if she didn't change her life soon she might end up seriously hurt or dead.

We found out recently that Terry Jo Howard has become a motivational speaker. Doing the interview for *Forensic Files* was one of the first times she spoke about her experience, and doing so was apparently something of a revelation. Hearing her own story made her want to tell it to other people. Telling her story got her to start speaking out about abuse. Now she speaks to women's groups across the country.

An interesting side note is that just before his arrest, James Randall had had a job replacing all the windows in the home of the lead forensic investigator's grandmother. The family had come to know him and thought he was a wonderful, personable guy. About a week after the job was finished the investigator got Randall's mug shot and called his grandmother to tell her that the nice man who fixed her windows was actually a serial sex-killer.

The "Treads and Threads" episode also featured an actress whose face is probably better known than her name. Zora Andrich played the part of one of the undercover detectives. She became known to TV viewers as the woman chosen by Joe Millionaire in the first of the popular series. One of her first acting gigs after she and the millionaire broke up was with us. She was a delight to work with, and is one of many young actors who've used our show as a stepping stone in their careers.

James Randall was sentenced to life in prison. You can see his picture on the website for the Florida Department of Corrections (http://www.dc.state.fl.us/). It's one of the best sites of its type in the country.

While a lot of the cases shown on *Forensic Files*—like the Randall case—feature new forensic techniques, we still do cases in which old-fashioned gumshoe work solves the crime.

In fact, one case actually caused us to view the word "gumshoe" in a whole new light. It was solved with a tiny piece of gum, no larger than a fingertip, and certainly belongs in the "Stranger than Fiction" category.

We called it "The Lasting Impression."

Her name was Richezza Williams, and her story is every parent's worst nightmare. Raised in a middle-class home in suburban New York, Richezza's teenage years were more rebellious than most. Just after her twelfth birthday she ran away from home and ended up in Easton, Pennsylvania, a small, historic city about ninety miles from New York City.

Richezza was smart, and resourceful. She supported herself running money and drugs for a New York based gang who called themselves "the Cash Money Brothers." To make sure her parents couldn't find her she took on a new identity. She changed her name to Materon Smith, and told people she was nineteen years old.

She became friends with a prostitute named Kathy Sagusti. Addicted to crack and down on her luck, the thirty-eight-year-old Sagusti took a maternal interest in her young friend. But she could do nothing when one day she saw three members of the Brothers attack her. Sagusti went to the police, but addled by her addiction and scared for her life, she couldn't give police enough to work with.

Days later the body of a young female turned up in what's known as a Dead House. You don't see them anymore, but as recently as a hundred years ago, Dead Houses, which are always on cemetery grounds, were used to store bodies during the winter. In the spring, when the ground thawed, the bodies were removed for proper burial.

Kathy Sagusti had told police that she thought the body might be that of Materon Smith, her nineteen-year-old friend. But when the forensic pathologist examined the body he found that the victim wasn't nineteen, she was in her early teens, perhaps twelve or thirteen. The cause of death was severe trauma to the head.

Police searched missing persons records for teenage runaways, and Richezza's faked identity was finally discovered. Sadly, it was too late for friends and family to do anything to help her. When police showed Kathy Sagusti a picture of Richezza she confirmed that it was the woman she knew as Materon Smith.

Police had a host of problems. Their only eyewitness to Richezza's alleged beating was Kathy Sagusti, and because of her drug addiction she was, at best, unreliable, especially in court. Still, police believed her story. They also thought the Cash Money Brothers had killed Richezza Williams, but they had to prove it. So they turned to one of the most reliable pieces of evidence available to a murder investigator: bugs.

The victim had been exposed for a number of days, plenty of time for fly larvae to infest the body. Dr. Neil Haskell, one of the country's most-respected "bug doctors"—forensic entomologists—was brought in to determine how old the fly larvae were. Since they grow at a predictable rate and will nest in a body within minutes of exposure, Dr. Haskell could tell investigators when the body had been dumped, and by doing so would give them a better idea when Richezza had been killed.

Dr. Haskell determined that the larvae on the body was five days old. Police noted that it was five days earlier that Kathy Sagusti said she'd seen the Cash Money Boys beating her friend. But police needed better evidence and went back to the Dead House to find it. They sifted through the dirt and debris around the spot where Richezza's body had been found. In the leaves, covered with dust, they found a tiny piece of discarded red chewing gum. At first glance it appeared there was some sort of impression in the gum.

Police gave the piece of gum to a forensic odontologist, Dr. Dennis Asen, who determined that it was in fact a remarkably good tooth impression. Perhaps even more significant, Dr. Asen indicated that the tooth seemed to have a unique chip, which might provide a match to a potential suspect.

Police decided to question Cory Mayweather, the leader of the Cash Money Boys. He joked with police, and said he had nothing to do with Richezza's murder. During questioning detectives got an unexpected surprise. Mayweather reached into his pocket and pulled out a packet of Big Red gum. He even offered some to detectives. They said no thanks, but did say they wanted a cast of Mayweather's teeth.

Dr. Asen made the cast and went over each tooth, painstakingly comparing every nook and cranny to the tooth impression from the tiny wad of gum found near Richezza's body. Even he thought the odds of finding a match were slim, but when he checked one of Mayweather's teeth he saw a unique piece of dental work. Mayweather had a cavity filled but the filling was chipped. Dr. Asen went back to the wad of gum and had trouble believing what he saw. The chip marks were identical. There was no doubt that Cory Mayweather's tooth had made the mark on the piece of gum recovered from the Dead House.

This put Mayweather at the scene of the murder. And when his defense lawyer was presented with the evidence he gave his client an unequivocal piece of advice: plead guilty and avoid the death penalty.

Cory Mayweather is now serving a life term, all because a tiny piece of gum proved beyond a doubt that he was the killer of a defenseless teenage runaway.

For the field producers of "The Lasting Impression," the case did exactly that—create a lasting impression. We shot extensive video at the actual Dead House where the body was found, a creepy experience for everyone involved. It was impossible to say how many bodies had been stored there—local historians said it was in the hundreds. But after hearing Richezza Williams's story—a teacher told us she was one of the brightest students she'd ever taught—it was disturbing to know we were in the same spot where she'd met her end.

This case was among the "greatest hits" in the career of the forensic odontologist, Dr. Asen. With our cameras rolling he re-created the process he used in the case, and proudly showed us the actual cast of Mayweather's teeth and a cast he'd made of the wad of gum found at the scene. The match was plainly visible to the naked eye. If you ever catch this episode, you will be able to see it clearly for yourself.

Dr. Asen's father was a police investigator, which is why he decided to have his dental practice branch out to include law enforcement. In fact Dr. Asen has such a passion for forensics that he's actually published a couple of detective stories from the point of view of a forensic odontologist. One of them is called *Root of Deception*, which goes to show that we're not the only people with a taste for puns in our titles.

Close watchers of the *Forensic Files* might notice that in "The Lasting Impression" episode, and a few others from the earlier cases, large sections are presented in black and white. It's actually 16 mm film. When we first began producing *Forensic Files*

Cory Mayweather. He could never have known that his fondness for chewing gum would land him in prison.

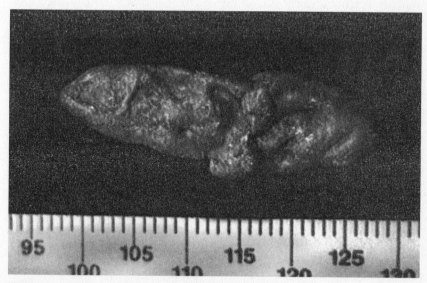

Evidence shot of Cory Mayweather's gum. Barely bigger than a thumb-nail, it contained a perfect impression of the killer's molars.

one of the fundamental questions we faced was exactly how we were going to go about re-creating the actual crimes. How much violence did we want to show? Would we need actors and actresses that bore a striking resemblance to their real-life counterparts? Did we want to match everything in the crime-scene photographs—the houses, the cars—even minor details like lamps and rugs?

Even more important—would the re-creations break up the continuity of the program? The re-creation section of each episode was what we began calling the "story within the story" and we had concerns that this sub-story within the actual program might turn people off, or might even confuse them.

Our initial solution was to let there be absolutely no doubt in the viewer's mind that the re-creations were in fact different than the rest of the show. And to do that one thing was absolutely vital: the re-creations needed to look different. So we turned to film.

Film leaves a completely different impression than video, a feature reinforced by our decision to use black and white. The texture of film provides some distance for the viewer with a slightly unreal quality, whereas video seems more real, more immediate, which is one of the reasons it's used in soap operas and many sitcoms. As a result, when the re-creations sections were cut into the show it became immediately clear that we had departed from the body of the program. To bring this departure home even further we almost always inserted a sound effect at the moment we switched from video to film. The sound, a sort of "swoosh" that lasted only about an eighth of a second, served to reinforce the idea that the story was going in a new direction.

We found this to be remarkably effective. In fact, it worked so well that many of the fictional forensic shows, like *CSI* and *Cold Case*, use something similar. They faced the same problem we did. At some point the actual story of what happened needed to be told, and some "effect" was needed to make this clear to the viewer. We found it interesting, and gratifying, that many of these shows hit upon the same solution.

These days regular *Forensic Files* viewers will notice that we no longer cut to black-and-white film. The reason? We discovered an even better solution. Recently developed video technology allows us to shoot the re-creations in color video, but with a "smearing" effect, in which an image lingers as a person or object moves, that still keeps these sections visually different than the rest of the show. The images have a dreamy quality that we think better serves the idea that we are traveling back to see what "really" happened when the crime was actually committed.

But for "The Lasting Impression" we used film. And getting the scene where the incriminating piece of gum fell from Cory Mayweather's mouth took hours. That's one of the difficulties of producing a program like this—the key visual elements are often no bigger than a penny; sometimes they're invisible to the naked eye.

It's amazing to think that something that small and seemingly insignificant can carry so much weight in a murder investigation. What's even stranger is that, thanks to advances in forensic technology, it's not uncommon.

Take, for instance, a story that certainly belongs in the Stranger than Fiction category. We named it "Line of Fire."

It began on April Fool's Day, 1996. A bomb exploded outside the office of a newspaper in Spokane, Washington. Luckily, no one was hurt, but there was no question that the bomb was designed to kill. When the smoke cleared, the bomb squad found a plastic bag near the building. Inside was a letter that began, "Greetings from Yahweh." The letter ended with a logo of sorts: a large letter "P" superimposed on a cross.

Shortly after the first explosion there was a second, this time at a local branch of the U.S. Bank. Two men set off the bomb after stealing $50,000. In their wake they left letters replete with biblical sayings and the same "P" logo.

Experts on domestic terrorism recognized the logo. It was from a group calling itself the Phineas Priests, a fundamentalist militia whose radical right-wing view of America was coupled with a conservative interpretation of scripture. The Priests fiercely opposed the U.S. government and were known for saying they wanted to destroy America in order to save it.

Three months after the first bombings the Priests struck again. This time a bomb exploded at a Planned Parenthood clinic. A nearby branch of the U.S. Bank was robbed a short time later. Residents of Spokane and the surrounding area were terrified. It was clear the Priests were willing to use deadly violence to achieve their goals. The fact that no one had been hurt was nothing short of a miracle.

A reward was offered for any information about the bombers, and in October an anonymous caller gave police the tip they'd been hoping for. The caller said the Priests were going to hit a U.S. bank branch in Portland, Oregon. He gave police the day and exact time of the planned robbery.

Police locked the bank doors and staked it out. At the time specified by the tipster three men—clad head-to-toe in masks and jackets—approached the bank. They banged on the doors, clearly frustrated and surprised that they couldn't get in. It was a regular business day and there would be no reason for the bank to be closed. Police followed them as they drove away and arrested them minutes later at a nearby gas station where they'd gone to change their clothes. The men were later found to be heavily armed, and their van was loaded with bomb materials and letters containing the telltale "P" logo.

It looked as if these were the men responsible for the wave

of bombings in Spokane, but surveillance photos of them as they robbed the banks appeared to be useless—the men were all wearing masks over their faces. Investigators needed more evidence, and when they searched the men's houses they found bomb-making materials and gunpowder that was later found to have the exact same chemical makeup as the powder used in the Spokane bombings.

Still, the FBI and government prosecutors wanted to make absolutely sure they had an airtight case. The types of people who would bomb their own country have utter contempt for the government. Prosecutors couldn't afford to lose the case. If they did it would only embolden these groups of home-grown terrorists and make them believe they could get away with future attacks. So investigators needed some rock-solid evidence to show jurors that the men they had in custody were the same men who were in the surveillance photos taken during the bank robberies.

To do this they made use of a pair of blue jeans found in the house of one of the suspects—something few would recognize as valuable evidence.

When Dr. Richard Voerder-Bruegge, a forensic video specialist with the FBI, saw the surveillance photographs of the bank robbery he quickly looked past the facial masks and shotguns. He looked at the jeans worn by one of the robbers. In the 35 mm surveillance image they were perfectly clear. When he enlarged the photos he could see a clear image of the seam running down the side of one pant leg and told prosecutors that, with luck, this would be as good as a fingerprint. They were skeptical, but needed hard evidence. They were curious to see if Dr. Voerder-Bruegge could deliver as promised.

Almost all blue jeans are made of white cotton that is then dyed blue. The dye wears off in distinctive patterns that are determined by the wearer's posture, how he or she walks, and a variety of other factors. One of the first places the dye wears off is along the seam and the cuffs. This creates what's known as a "hill and valley" effect. The areas closest to the surface turn white faster than areas below the creases, and those areas retain the blue dye.

In looking at the robbery photographs Dr. Voerder-Bruegge thought one of the robbers was one of the men in custody, Charles Barbee—they appeared to be the same height and build. Dr. Voerder-Bruegge asked investigators to give him every pair of jeans they could find in Barbee's home. He then photographed the seams along Barbee's jeans and compared them to blow-ups of the jeans worn by the robber in the surveillance photograph.

In one pair of jeans a pattern was clearly visible—the "hill and valley" pattern along the seam was exactly the same as the pattern in the jeans worn by the robber. In a process known as "point-by-point analysis," Dr. Voerder-Bruegge used blow-ups of the photos to show beyond a doubt that the jeans worn by the robber in the bank surveillance photos were the same pair of jeans confiscated from Charles Barbee's home. Even though Barbee had done everything possible to conceal his identity, he could never have known that his jeans would give him away.

For his part, Dr. Voerder-Bruegge was only too happy to talk to us about the case. He joked about his appearance on the witness stand. "I testified that I couldn't say for certain it was Charles Barbee in that bank surveillance photograph," he told us, "but they were definitely his jeans. And how's he going to explain that a bank robber he doesn't even know somehow got a hold of his pants?" That, apparently, was the same question asked by jurors, who convicted Charles Barbee and his two conspirators, resulting in mandatory life sentences.

This case was one of many we've done with the assistance of the FBI, home to one of the finest forensic laboratories in the

A bank surveillance photo of the April Fool's bank robbery. Forget the mask. The robber's pants identified him.

world. Processing evidence requires vast amounts of patience, and to watch FBI analysts spend hours scraping a blanket for bits of trace evidence or crawling over every inch of a suspect's vehicle is to know how seriously they take every single case. Evidence is sent to them from all over the world. They know that somewhere a grieving family member is desperate for closure, and that their handling of the evidence could make the difference between a killer facing justice or a killer going free.

A show like *Forensic Files* wouldn't be possible without the help of people like the FBI and law enforcement professionals from all over the world. That they're fans of the show not only makes it easier for us to produce it, it makes it a lot more gratifying.

In the case called "Line of Fire" the FBI rolled out the red carpet. Dr. Voerder-Bruegge took us through each step of the process that led to matching the jeans. It took him weeks to enlarge the surveillance photographs and do all his comparisons. Given the constraints of television we condensed this process to about two minutes, but if you ever catch the episode you'll see how the jeans match—it's as clear as day.

Another problem on this particular story was simulating the bombings and the bank robberies. Businesses who happen to be near the *Forensic Files* production office are used to having us around. What that means is fairly regular requests to blow up smoke bombs in their lobbies, or have masked men rush through their foyers with fake, but real-looking weapons.

Whenever we do something like this we tell the surrounding businesses what we'll be up to, and we call the local police to tell them "no, we're not actually robbing the bank at the corner of 4th and Hamilton." Still, there have been problems, and "Line of Fire" was a case in point.

We had two actors, faces covered in masks, and clad head-to-toe in anything that could be used to conceal their identity. And our prop man, thanks again to his art school training, had made us a series of propped-up pipe bombs. They looked just like the real thing and when lighted they would fizz and smoke, but, of course, would not blow up.

That did not convince one local accountant whose coworkers failed to tell him what we were doing. When he saw two masked men light a bomb and run away, he called police in a panic. (Our re-creation camera is so small and so lightweight he apparently thought it was a gun, or perhaps another bomb.) They came to the site with sirens blaring, only to find out that it was their favorite production company up to its usual tricks. They've become used to us, and we do everything we can to warn them, but occasionally something slips through the cracks. Police, especially these days, can never be too careful, and when someone claims there's a bomber in their lobby the police seem to think it's best to err on the side of caution, and we certainly can't argue with that. Luckily, they're usually more amused than angry. And that's a good thing, because we're constantly asking them if we can use their police cars and interrogation rooms for re-creations.

Perhaps the strangest case we've had that simply defies belief is one with what is probably the strangest title of any of our almost two hundred episodes. We called it "Killigraphy" and more than one of the people we interviewed commented that if this story were submitted to Hollywood it would get rejected for being too far-fetched. Decide for yourself.

The most obvious suspect is all too often the guilty party in a crime, and sometimes a suspect is so unappealing that the community assumes the suspect is guilty. The physical evidence doesn't always cooperate in our assumptions, however, and can prove the innocence of even the most appealing and most obvious suspect.

Alvin Ridley was the local television repair man in Ringgold, Georgia, a small, one-horse town located at the base of the Blue Ridge Mountains. In 1975, Alvin's father was in an accident while driving Alvin's van. Because of the legal fees surrounding the accident which had not been paid, Alvin's van was confiscated in 1984. This incident and his father's death in 1988 was the apparent impetus for Alvin's downward spiral into paranoia and seclusion.

His erratic behavior caused people in the small town to refer to him as "Crazy Alvin." There was talk that he held his wife captive in his ramshackle, dilapidated house. Alvin also started to write letters to government agencies citing alleged social injustices, stemming, many believe, from what he saw as the unfair confiscation of his van.

Then the real trouble began. On October 4, 1997, Alvin said he found his wife, Virginia, lying face down in her bed, apparently unconscious. Alvin did not call the local ambulance and rescue squad. Instead, he called a Chattanooga, Tennessee, hospital that was ten miles out of town. They, in turn, called local authorities.

The local EMTs and the Catoosa County Coroner arrived at Alvin's cockroach-infested shack. They found Virginia's dead body in a room filled with urine and excrement.

After about thirty hours at the Coroner's office, the body was taken to the Georgia Bureau of Investigation Crime Lab where an autopsy was performed. Virginia Ridley's cause of death was listed as asphyxiation. The official ruling was that she had been murdered, and Alvin was soon charged with killing his wife. No one in the town of Ringgold was surprised by this charge. They all thought Alvin, who had made numerous threats on town residents, was potentially dangerous.

Police, now considering a charge of murder, looked more deeply into Alvin's background.

They found that in 1967, Virginia Ridley's family filed court papers in order to see their daughter. They hadn't seen or heard from her in years, and were concerned about her well-being. Virginia appeared in court and said she was fine, and that she simply wanted to be left alone. Family members told them that they had gone to the house to see Virginia, only to be threatened by Alvin. When questioned by police he said he was following his wife's wishes.

The body of Virginia Ridley yielded various clues as to the manner of her death. There was evidence of neck muscle hemorrhaging—a sign of strangulation. Virginia's eyes and face exhibited another sign of strangulation, petechiae, and Tardieu spots. Both are red-spotting caused by broken blood vessels. The last sign of foul play was what looked to be a ligature mark on her wrist, and some bruising around her neck. To many this fueled the rumor that Virginia was being held captive by Alvin, and that he'd finally strangled her to death.

After six months of investigation, the District Attorney felt he had enough evidence to charge Alvin with murder.

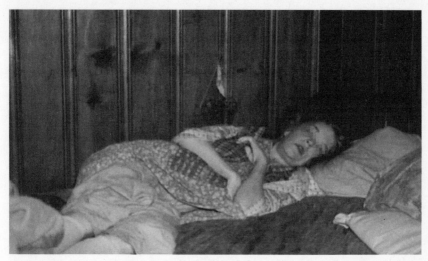

Virginia Ridley in death. Did she die peacefully or as the victim of pre-meditated violence?

Local papers branded Alvin as a small-town eccentric, and it was the general consensus of the townspeople that Alvin was a murderer. They wondered why he would bypass the local ambulances to call on a hospital ten miles away. He was reported to have been upset when there was mention of an autopsy on Virginia. The unsanitary conditions in which Alvin and Virginia lived also did nothing to help his reputation.

Only one person believed in Alvin's innocence, attorney McCraken "Ken" Poston. Ken Poston called Dr. Robert Goldberg, a forensic investigator with degrees in psychology, law, and medicine. Dr. Goldberg read the autopsy report and asked to see the crime scene photos.

Dr. Goldberg was shocked to learn that only four photos had been taken at the crime scene, and that there were no photos taken at the autopsy. Dr. Goldberg asked that the original photos be enlarged, and these pictures told a tale of misconduct and mistaken medical facts.

The prosecution's basic contention was that Virginia had

been strangled to death. They maintained that the blood found in the muscles of the neck and the red-spotting in her eyes and on her face could have only resulted from her being strangled.

In photos of the body taken at the home there were no signs of this spotting, which, in the case of a strangulation death, would have appeared immediately. Because of this Dr. Goldberg concluded that strangulation could not have been the cause of death. To prove this he needed to find out why these marks were not present at the alleged crime scene but were present at the autopsy. He believed something happened to the body *after* death.

In one of the photos Dr. Goldberg saw the coroner rotating Virginia Ridley's upper body. Such movement of a body shortly after death would cause blood to drain into the extremities. This led him to conclude that some of the spotting was what's known as "artifact," a term for any changes to the body caused by post-mortem evaluation. However, artifact could not account for all of the spotting.

In checking Virginia's medical history Dr. Goldberg found that she had epilepsy. A characteristic of this disease is the grand mal seizure, in which an electrical short-circuit in the brain causes all breathing to stop. If Virginia had such a seizure it could account for the spotting appearing later—after the photos were taken. A strangulation death with its violent cessation of breathing would cause blood vessels to burst, and would result in the spotting. A seizure would produce a similar result, but since it would not be as violent, the spotting would take considerably longer to appear.

The next question was the marks on the neck that indicated strangulation. An investigation revealed that the coroner who did the initial evaluation drew blood from Virginia's neck for toxicology tests. Such a procedure is highly unusual; blood for a test like that is usually drawn from the arm. This did, however, explain the marks on the neck: there is less muscle in this area, and a needle would have left a mark consistent with the one found on Virginia Ridley.

The alleged ligature marks on Virginia's wrist were also suspicious. Family members told Dr. Goldberg that she never took off her wedding ring or watch. Dr. Goldberg concluded that the watch had been removed after the initial investigation. What this meant was that the marks could have been caused by post-mortem blood coagulation around the watch-marks—that shortly after death blood drained into the area that was once constricted by the watchband. As the body cooled the blood stayed there, giving the impression of a ligature mark. Dr. Goldberg told investigators this was very common and said it should have been obvious to the coroner.

But Alvin's detractors—those in town who said he was crazy—described him as violent and were convinced he was capable of murder. Alvin's defense needed to show that he loved his wife and would do nothing to harm her. In the home they found key pieces of evidence—something that had never turned up in any murder investigation on record. The home contained love notes—by the thousand. These notes, written by Virginia to Alvin, were found in every room in the house, many of them taped to the walls. Handwriting analysis proved the letters were written by Virginia. Scientists said they were further proof of her epilepsy, *and* further proof that Alvin didn't kill her.

Due to her condition Virginia suffered from something called hypergraphia, an uncommon but not unknown side-effect of epilepsy. Sufferers of hypergraphia write incessantly about the trivial details of their daily life, and in some cases will spend most of their waking hours writing. All indications were that this was the case with Virginia Ridley. In every note found in the house Virginia professed her love for Alvin; at no point did she write anything indicating unhappiness in her

marriage. Epilepsy experts said that if she had been unhappy—
if she had felt in any way threatened by her husband—she
would not have been able to resist the compulsion to write
about it.

Dr. Goldberg concluded that Virginia's death was due to
asphyxia, caused by a grand mal epileptic seizure. He learned
from Alvin that on the day prior to Virginia's death she suffered from a long grand mal seizure. Often in severe epileptic
seizures, this is a precursor to the fatal attack. Dr. Goldberg told
investigators Virginia had not been murdered, but died of natural causes—that the epileptic seizure created a false appearance of strangulation, and that post-mortem handling of the
body caused the suspect bruising.

Faced with this evidence, all charges against Alvin Ridley
were dropped. He still lives in Ringgold, and his neighbors still
refer to him as "Crazy Alvin." But, without the work of a committed defense lawyer and some top-notch forensic science,
Alvin would most likely have been convicted of a crime that
never even happened.

In almost any television show time constraints make it
impossible to include every single fact and anecdote. And
sometimes it's painful for producers to leave choice bits of a
story "on the floor," as the saying goes. The Alvin Ridley story
is a case in point; there was simply so much "story," and so
much science that some of the sidebars never made the show.

For instance, Alvin's house was a filthy wreck, and if you
ever see the show this will become immediately obvious. There
are holes in the floor and in the walls; there are flies buzzing
around half-eaten and half-rotted plates of food. There are
some types of stains (we still don't know what they are) on the
living room floor. Alvin did not make any concessions to the
TV crew that was coming over to put his place on national television. The place was dirtier and more rundown than any we
had ever seen.

And he didn't do much to help himself when he finally made an appearance in court. Some days he would show up in a neck brace; others without it. When asked if he'd been injured, he refused to answer.

He provided only limited cooperation to his lawyer. There were documents related to his marriage and his wife's medical condition that he would never let out of his sight. He kept them in a battered briefcase and would only let his lawyer, Ken Poston, examine them when he was present. Poston had agreed to take on the case pro bono because he was convinced Alvin was being railroaded and would not be adequately defended by a court-appointed lawyer. He mounted a vigorous defense, but still, Alvin would not let him alone with the briefcase and the documents.

One day, Alvin brought the briefcase to court. And we'll let Ralph Van Pelt, the judge who presided over the case take the story from here. This is a part of the transcript of our interview that didn't make the show.

Judge Van Pelt: "It's a little bit unusual for somebody to have physical evidence that would help their defense and then not give it to their lawyer.

Producer: "And when he opened the suitcases in the courtroom, you had a little problem. Is that right?"

Judge Van Pelt: "Mm-mm, well a few problems. I mean obviously uh ongoing little problem with smell and then occasionally a, uh as time went by and things I guess the, we were doing this in January and, it obviously was probably cold in Alvin's house, but once it was uh brought here and opened up and sat around for a few days some things started hatching, yes.

Producer: "I'm not sure I understand. What exactly are we talking about?"

Judge Van Pelt: "Well, roaches."

Producer: "Roaches? So he was bringing in the suitcases and—?"

Judge Van Pelt: "Yeah, the eggs were hatching off the, I guess the paper, and the paperwork and some of the other things they brought in, yeah."

Producer: "So you had little crawlies in your courtroom?"

Judge Van Pelt: "Well, I didn't ever have one get to me, but occasionally I'd hear the sound of someone (audible foot stomping) getting rid of one."

Producer: "And I heard it got pretty bad."

Judge Van Pelt: "Well, it didn't get distracting. It was, it was just one more weird thing for a not uh quite usual trial, yeah. It never got to the point where I felt it was distracting. The jury, I don't know if they even, they even noticed, but you'd occasionally hear a bailiff or a deputy or someone sitting in the front of the courtroom stomp a cockroach, but that was about it."

Producer: "It sounds a little weird . . ."

Judge Van Pelt: "Mm, a little different, yes."

A little different is an appropriately "judicious" way to describe it. As we say, you can't make some of this stuff up. Someone who knew Alvin told us before we shot his interview that things would go much more smoothly if we had a woman on the production team. This person said that Alvin could sometimes get hostile to men, but if an attractive woman were on board he would be as "docile as a cat." We took this advice to heart, gave our regular soundman the day off, and made some calls to some friendly production companies in nearby cities. A young, attractive female sound technician arrived the next day and, as predicted, Alvin was the picture of charm and southern hospitality.

We're told that Alvin is alive and well and still in the same house. Whether it's with roaches or not, we can't say; he still doesn't like to open the place to strangers.

THREE
Shooting the Lie

Most everyone who works for *Forensic Files* came to the program with a background in news. That meant we had fairly extensive dealings with the criminal justice system, but nothing had prepared any of us for dealing with individual cases in such depth. There's a saying in television that ten seconds is "an eternity." That's true, and it's something we'd all lived for most of our careers. So you can imagine that we paused a little when faced with the prospect of doing an entire half-hour on a single story.

The learning curve was steep, to say the least. We had to have the details of the cases we had chosen down cold. If we didn't, the prosecutors and homicide detectives wouldn't take us seriously, and besides, we'd never be able to get the story to the air with the proper degree of accuracy. We weren't experts in forensic science, and so we hit the books, and we hit them hard.

Still, even with all that preparation we faced some unexpected hurdles as we began producing the show. One of the strangest is what we now call "shooting the lie."

When a killer tries to cover up his tracks—when he tries to conceal his involvement in the murder from investigators—he essentially creates a lie. Forensic scientists try to expose those lies, and we've found that, for certain stories, the viewer must see the lie to understand how it was finally exposed as fake. So there have been a number of times when we've actually re-created and filmed the killer's fake story. When we started producing *Forensic Files* we didn't have a name for this. Now we call it "shooting the lie."

The first time we did it was for an infamous case out of Texas, a case we called "The Invisible Intruder."

In June 1996, police in a Dallas suburb got an emergency call from a woman in panic. Her name was Darlie Routier. She said she had fallen asleep on a downstairs couch while her six-year-old son Devon and his five-year-old brother Damon slept on the floor in front of the TV. Darlie later told investigators that she awoke to find an intruder standing over her. The man became startled and fled toward a utility room. Darlie said she heard glass breaking as he ran away. She ran in the direction the man had fled, and armed herself with a large kitchen knife she found on the floor of the kitchen. As she picked up the knife she said she realized her clothing—a white T-shirt—was covered in blood. Thinking the intruder was in the garage she ran back into the house to call her husband, Darin, who was sleeping upstairs.

Darin Routier came downstairs to find one of the most horrific crime scenes in Texas history. His two sons had been stabbed repeatedly. One was already dead; the other died shortly afterward on the way to the hospital. Blood drenched the living room-floor. Darlie had a slash wound on her neck and some cuts on her arm. Luckily, an infant son, asleep upstairs, was unhurt.

As paramedics and police processed the scene, Darin Routier said one of the strangest things local homicide investigators had ever heard. Minutes after the brutal murder of his two oldest sons, he turned to Detective Chris Frosh and said, "My wife is so beautiful. She has 38 double-D breasts."

Things would soon get even stranger. Nothing in the house was stolen, even though a jewelry box was in plain sight. Darlie had not been sexually assaulted, and even if the killer had meant to rape her he had, for some unknown reason, decided to attack the boys first.

Further, there were no foreign fingerprints in the house. The window screen in the garage was cut open, but no fingerprints were found there, and the dust under the window was undisturbed. If this was how the killer had gained entry to the house, he had done so without leaving a single mark.

Tom Bevel, an expert in blood spatter analysis, was called to the scene. Since both boys had bled to death he found literally quarts of blood in the living room and the adjoining area. In the kitchen he noticed a vacuum cleaner which had been knocked over. There was blood on the grip, which clearly indicated someone had handled the vacuum cleaner either during or after the attack. There was also blood on the wheels, and bloody tracks indicating the vacuum cleaner had been moved back and forth.

DNA analysis revealed the blood on the grip and the wheels belonged to Darlie Routier.

Bevel then examined the white T-shirt Darlie was wearing during the attack. She had sustained cuts to the neck and arms and most of the blood was hers. But on the front shoulder and on the back were some strange bloodstains. They had "tails," which to an analyst like Tom Bevel indicated they had been cast-off, which is to say "thrown" on to the shirt from a bloody hand, or possibly, a bloody knife.

DNA analysis revealed these cast-off blood spatters and Darlie's T-shirt were the boys' blood.

The kitchen was processed with Luminol. By reacting with iron it reveals human blood even after all visible traces have been removed. The Luminol revealed a trail of bare footprints from the living room to the kitchen. The footprints stopped at the kitchen sink. There was also blood on the sink and countertop.

The footprints matched Darlie Routier's feet, and DNA showed the blood was hers.

An analysis of the screen in the garage that had been cut open revealed it was cut from the inside—that whoever had cut it was in the house at the time. And microscopic analysis of all the knives in the kitchen revealed that one knife—which had been replaced in the butcher block—had been used to cut the screen.

It was clear to investigators that there was no intruder. The evidence showed that it was Darlie Routier who had killed her own sons. The story it told was that Darlie had grabbed a knife from the kitchen butcher block and used it to cut the screen in the garage. She then replaced that knife and grabbed another from the same block. She used this to stab her sons to death. While she was stabbing them, cast-off spatters from the blood-soaked knife stained her white T-shirt. The footprints and bloodstains showed she walked to the kitchen sink, and this explained the wounds she sustained. Heavy drops of blood, indicating it came from a stationary object, were on the floor. Darlie had stood at the kitchen sink and slashed her neck and arms. Darlie needed those wounds to make it appear that an outside intruder was in fact the killer.

Wound analysis later proved the wounds were self-inflicted.

Sometime before police arrived, Darlie broke some wine

Evidence photo of Darlie Routier. Note the slash on the throat. Self-inflicted or the work of an enraged killer? Or both?

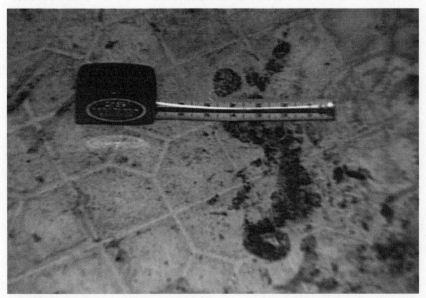

Evidence photo of a bloody footprint on the Routiers' kitchen floor, the only foreign footprint in the house.

glasses and toppled over the vacuum cleaner to make it look as if there had been a struggle. In doing so, she placed her own bloodstains on the handle of the vacuum cleaner.

This and other evidence indicated that the intruder certainly was "invisible." He was so invisible that he didn't exist.

Police needed a motive. They soon found out that the Routiers had been falling into debt and had to curtail their fairly lavish lifestyle. Darlie was apparently unwilling to do this and decided that with two of her sons out of the way she could continue to live in the style to which she'd become accustomed.

Darlie was put under surveillance and days later a controversial videotape was made as she and her husband stood at the graveside of their murdered sons. Darlie held an impromptu birthday party for young Devon Routier. She sprayed silly string around the grave and sang the boys' favorite song, which reinforced the impression that she was glad to be free of them.

She was arrested shortly afterward and was later found guilty of two counts of first-degree murder. She now sits on death row, where she still maintains her innocence. The case continues to generate controversy and we got hate-mail from as far away as Germany after our program aired. Despite overwhelming evidence many people insist Darlie Routier is innocent.

When covering this case, the main question for us was how to show the elaborate cover-up on the part of the killer. A debate ensued between some production staff who wanted to stick to a traditional news-oriented approach and not show the fake story. They thought that doing so would be confusing since we were essentially putting "false" information on the screen. Others disagreed. They said that, at least in the early part of the investigation, the fake story was very real to prosecutors who had to deal with it as fact until it could be verified or disproved by the evidence. Their argument was that if we were going to view the investigation through the eyes of the actual investigators the fake story had to be shown.

Finally that argument prevailed and we all agreed that the only way to present the case properly was to re-create Darlie Routier's version of the story. She claimed an intruder did it, so we decided we would show the murder from the intruder's point of view. We had no idea of the difficulties we would encounter.

After two days of shooting, the re-creations director came back to the edit suite with the footage. He was met with consternation by the producers. They said it didn't "work," that it was disjointed and impossible to cut together because it didn't make sense. The re-creations director tried again—at great expense. But, again, there were the same problems.

We all sat down to look at the footage. What was going on? And suddenly we realized what it was, and that's when we came up with the phrase "shooting the lie."

The problem was that the lie itself—Darlie's fake story—made no sense. The lie had no internal logic of its own; it didn't exist in real life and was impossible to re-create in a way that looked credible on-camera.

Try it for yourself. Here are the questions that have to be answered for the "intruder" story to hold up:

The intruder has to enter the home (*how?*). Once inside he has to cut the garage screen from the inside and then replace the knife (*why?*), he has to attack the boys *before* attacking Darlie (*why?*), and then, after the murders, he has to inflict a superficial wound on Darlie (*why, if he was willing to kill the boys, was he unwilling to kill her?*). Finally, on the way out of the house he has to grab the vacuum cleaner and move it around on the floor before toppling it over (*again, why?*). This scenario does not even attempt to answer questions of how Darlie's sons' cast-off blood spatters got on her shirt, why her bloody footprints lead to the kitchen sink, and why large drops of her blood were found there in a cluster.

This was our first experience with shooting a killer's false story, and it was a lesson we never forgot. It also saved the re-creations director a lot of subsequent grief. No longer would he be responsible for trying to impose logic on a story that had no logic of its own.

This, however, didn't make things any easier, especially when the killer's story turned out to be utterly preposterous. Killers who plan things out ahead of time can usually antici-pate some of what investigators will do. When they concoct their lie after the murder, they have to do it "on the fly" and they find themselves in deep trouble. Take the case of a Seattle area police officer, a case we called "Burning Ambition."

On August 10, 1996, King County Police received a call about a domestic disturbance in a Seattle suburb. Thirty-five-year-old James Christopher Wren had gotten into a shouting match with his housemate, Emmett Marcel. It was not the first time there had been such a disturbance; just weeks earlier Emmett Marcel had shot Wren in the leg during a similar alter-cation. In fact, Wren had a cast on his leg from that shooting.

The policeman sent to the scene told neighbors he was escorting Wren to the local substation to get a statement. The last anyone ever saw of James Wren was as he was driven off in a King County patrol car, his spray-painted leg cast propped up on the back seat.

When Wren didn't return home that night or the following day his family informed police. They were told that Wren gave his statement and was released. He was known for being some-thing of an indigent and, since his domestic situation was so unstable, many people thought he was just staying with friends until the situation cooled down. The possibility that he had just left town was also considered.

But weeks went by and nothing was heard from him. Police began to consider the possibility of foul play. Wren was known to be an associate of one Jesus Hernandez, a convicted drug dealer. Wren's roommate, Emmett Marcel, had a history of mental disturbance and had recently shot him in the leg. Neighbors said they had heard Emmett Marcel threaten to kill Wren if Wren told police who had shot him.

But the questioning of Jesus Hernandez brought some interesting information. He told them that the officer who had taken Wren's statement, King County Police Sergeant Matt Bachmeier, had recently tried to shake him down for $50,000 after a drug bust. Hernandez said Bachmeier was a dirty cop and might be setting him up as a fall-guy for Wren's disappearance.

Bachmeier was a twenty-five-year veteran of the police force and was well-liked and respected. But in July 1996, just one month before Wren's disappearance, Bachmeier's house had burned down. An investigation revealed the cause as arson. Bachmeier had an alibi for the night in question, but police could find no other suspects and their investigation always led back to him.

Bachmeier said he thought the arsonist was someone he'd arrested years earlier and who was now on the streets—a dealer named "Rios." In fact, on the door of a garage untouched by the fire, someone had spray-painted the words "Rios Lives" and "Your Dead." The misspelling of "your" was not considered significant at the time, but it was still early in the investigation.

But if Sgt. Bachmeier was the arsonist, what was the motive? He collected almost $150,000 in insurance and it was known that he had ambitions to quit his job. He had tired of being a policeman and wanted to pursue his lifelong ambition: professional bowling. Valuable items had also been removed from the house before it burned down and these were still in Bachmeier's possession. These included all his bowling trophies and his prized collection of porcelain pigs (we're not kidding).

For seasoned arson investigators, this was a red flag. It

sounds strange, but a large percentage of people who torch their own homes will often remove heirlooms and other valuables and try to hide them away. In addition, a neighbor had seen a man resembling Bachmeier on a motorcycle just before the fire started, but since the man was wearing a helmet she couldn't be completely sure who it was.

With Wren nowhere to be found, and with Bachmeier apparently the last person to have seen him alive, police decided to check out the admittedly unlikely possibility that he could have had anything to do with Wren's disappearance. When questioned, Bachmeier presented a piece of evidence that would affect both his arson case the case of James Wren: a five-page confession, apparently signed by Wren, in which Wren admitted burning down Bachmeier's house. This was unusual, to say the least, and police looked on this connection between Wren and Bachmeier as more than a coincidence. So they took an even closer look at their fellow officer.

When they searched the back of Bachmeier's patrol car they found what looked to be blood; traces were also found on his shoes, his camera bag, and a briefcase he kept in the back of his car. A considerable effort had been made to clean this blood.

Reverse paternity testing of the DNA found in the blood indicated it was Wren's. Faced with this evidence Bachmeier told police an interesting story, a story that turned out to be an incredibly elaborate lie.

He admitted that he had tried to shake down Wren and Jesus Hernandez for $50,000 after finding them with methamphetamine. He said that both men had threatened revenge. Bachmeier was convinced it was Wren and Hernandez who had burned down his home. He said he confronted Wren on the night of his arrest and had obtained a five page confession—in Wren's handwriting—admitting responsibility for the arson. He theorized that Wren had left town after giving the confession to avoid facing charges. He explained away the blood in the back of his car by saying that Wren had been bloodied during the domestic disturbance and had deposited the blood while sitting in the car.

This didn't wash with police investigators. First, there was enough blood traces in the back of the car to indicate that Wren had suffered a major—possibly fatal—injury. A handwriting analysis of the "confession" indicated it was not Wren's writing. A compositional analysis of the language revealed something interesting. At least four times in the confession the writer used the word "your" when he meant to use the contraction "you're." Analysis of Wren's previous writings indicated he never made this mistake. The same analysis of things Sgt. Bachmeier had written showed he often made this mistake.

And this same "mistake" was spray-painted on Bachmeier's garage door. The arsonist hadn't written "You're Dead," he had written "Your Dead," and this was consistent with the spelling error made numerous times by Sgt. Bachmeier.

It was hard to deny the facts, even if they defied belief. Bachmeier was charged with Wren's murder, and with torching his own house. His defense lawyers scoffed. They said there was no body and that their client's story made perfect sense. For them, the lack of a body proved not that Wren was dead but that he had run away—a scenario they described as eminently plausible, or at least plausible enough to establish reasonable doubt in the eyes of a jury. Furthermore, they said the reverse-paternity testing of the DNA was not definitive; prosecutors could only say the blood might be Wren's and nothing more. They added that Sgt. Bachmeier had a stellar record and was financially solvent—he would have no motive to burn his house down for insurance and then kill someone to cover it up.

Jousting between both sides continued for six months after Wren's disappearance. Then, in February 1997, a hiker in the Cougar Mountain Park found a skeleton. When he called

police he said he found part of a leg covered with a spray paint-
ed cast, which set off alarm bells for those familiar with the
Bachmeier case. The skeleton was soon identified as James
Christopher Wren's.

The discovery of the body put to rest any rumors that Wren
had simply run away. The case went to trial. Bachmeier's lawyers again claimed there were any number of people who
could have killed Wren: perhaps his drug dealer friends or even
his mentally unstable roommate. After all, he had already shot
him once and threatened to kill him.

But the prosecution put together a web of circumstantial evidence. The DNA and the amount of blood in Bachmeier's car
made it likely that Wren had been killed there. The handwriting analysis indicated Wren was not the author. The compositional analysis—the consistent misspelling of "your"—confirmed this and pointed to Bachmeier.

Prosecutors told jurors a seemingly incredible story. They
said that Bachmeier, worried because he knew he would likely
be charged with arson, was desperate to present police with
another suspect. When he was called to Wren's house to investigate the domestic disturbance he thought he had found his
man: a drifter with a previous record and a history of being
attacked. Prosecutors said Bachmeier cooked up the confession
to make it appear that Wren was the arsonist, then killed him
and disposed of his body. Finally, to take suspicion away from
himself, he told police that Wren must have run away to avoid
facing an arson charge.

After six hours of deliberation a jury found Matt Bachmeier
guilty of first-degree murder and sentenced him to life in
prison.

As you can see, Sgt. Bachmeier was making it up as he went
along, which is why his story fell apart after the tiniest bit of
scrutiny. But what was good news for prosecutors was a nightmare for us. What we ended up with was another case of hav-

ing to "shoot the Lie," but in this case the lie was so outlandish we ran the risk of confusing viewers by showing it. Even we had trouble keeping some of it straight.

The solution was to use one of the oldest and, some would say hackneyed, effects in the television lexicon: the wipe. It is exactly what the term indicates—an effect that essentially "wipes" the screen and by doing so makes it clear to the viewer that they are being taken to a new area of the story. Wipes come in a variety of shapes and sizes. Sometimes a circle, a square, or a star will wipe the screen. Other times a bar will move from left to right to do the same thing. Since viewers these days are more accustomed to disjoined story lines than they were as recently as ten years ago, you don't see wipes as much as you used to. They're popular in soap operas, but rarely create problems because soap opera viewers are already familiar with the characters and the story line.

In this case we had no such luxury. A typical *Forensic Files* episode is, first of all, based on real events, and that provides a host of constraints. There's an old adage in newsrooms around the world—"don't let the facts get in the way of a good story"—and it's used as a warning to reporters who might be tempted to fidget with details to make their story "cleaner" or more accessible. At *Forensic Files* we have to let the "facts get in the way" because if we didn't the law enforcement community wouldn't take us seriously and would stop cooperating with us. In addition, almost all of us are journalists and we approach each story as journalism first and entertainment second.

So, if you watch the "Burning Ambition" episode you'll see something you rarely see in one our stories: wipe after wipe after wipe. It was the only way to tell Sgt. Bachmeier's incredible lie without having the story veer off into some sort of TV never-never-land. After all, Bachmeier claimed he did a shakedown on Wren and his friend; he claimed Wren willingly signed the confession; he claimed Wren was able to return to his home after only superficial injuries; he claimed someone else torched his house.

Even with the wipes in place we feared Bachmeier's lie was so elaborate it would be impossible to follow. So, we came up with an unusual plan. We made VHS copies of the "rough-cut" of the program and four of the people working on the show brought these home to show to their families. The families had no prior knowledge of the case. They would be our "jury": if they couldn't follow the story we would have to come up with another way to tell it.

To our considerable relief the verdict was in our favor. Everyone said they could follow it, and they even held up under post-viewing "interrogation." We asked them questions about the case and everyone was clear on who was who and which story was the "lie" and which story was the actual fact.

Sgt. Bachmeier's story was described by those investigating his case as one of the "dumbest" they'd ever heard. We'd have a hard time disagreeing, but it certainly presented one of the more unusual challenges we'd ever been faced with, and to this day it remains one of our all-time favorite episodes.

It sometimes seems that the more preposterous the story the more problems it presents, at least in terms of shooting the perpetrator's "lie." One of the most unusual—and most outlandish—stories we were ever presented with concerned a bona fide black widow in rural North Carolina. We called it, appropriately, "Broken Promises."

On February 1, 1988, a young boy made a frantic call to 911 dispatchers in Durham County, North Carolina. On the verge of hysteria, the little boy told the dispatcher that his father needed help. The dispatcher asked what had happened, and the child replied, "He had a gun and it went off."

Among the first to arrive at the house was Doug Griffin, a member of the local volunteer fire department, who lived only a few blocks away. Griffin was taken into the upstairs bedroom, where he found a dying Russ Stager, a man he'd known for years.

Russ Stager was a popular coach at Durham High School, a revered figure to his students and fellow teachers, many of whom described him as self-effacing—to a fault. He was married to Barbara Stager, a second marriage for the both of them. The Stagers were popular, active members in the Baptist community of Durham. Barbara had two sons from her previous marriage. Russ treated the boys as if they were his own, and eventually adopted them.

About forty minutes after the 911 call, Russ was rushed to Duke University Medical Center, but his condition was critical: he had sustained a massive head wound. Shortly after his arrival, doctors told the family that Russ was brain dead. For a few agonizing minutes the family was torn: should they keep him alive on life-support or let him die. They decided against any artificial means to prolong his life, and Russ died three hours after being taken off life support.

Russ's wife, Barbara, told police that, despite her protests, Russ kept a loaded gun under his pillow for protection. She had heard her son get up to use the bathroom, and she was concerned that Russ might think there was a prowler in the house, so she went to retrieve the gun from under the pillow. But when she reached under the pillow, the gun accidentally went off, firing the fatal shot into the back of his head.

Sergeant Rich Buchanan went to the Stagers' home to determine if further investigation was required. Barbara's father, James Terry, came out of the house with the bloodied sheets and pillowcases left from the accident. Terry asked Buchanan if he needed the sheets, and Buchanan said no, since it appeared the shooting was an accident.

But he soon began to change his mind. Barbara was calm and took Buchanan to the shooting scene without hesitation or emotion. Buchanan was feeling uneasy, and his instincts told him that something was amiss. In his years on the job he'd never seen someone so composed so soon after the untimely death of a loved one.

Later that night, Russ's first wife, Jo Lynn, arrived home. The two had remained close despite their divorce, and talked to each other at least a couple of times a month. When Jo Lynn heard of Russ's death, she felt she needed to speak to police, and the next day Sergeant Buchanan heard an unusual story.

Jo Lynn said that Russ was suspicious—even scared—of Barbara. He said she was having affairs and not being discreet about it. He said that large sums of money were missing from their joint accounts, and that, when asked, Barbara refused to say how it was spent. But perhaps most disturbing was that she had made up a story about being offered a huge book deal. The book was supposedly about the untimely death of her first husband, which Russ now believed was not an accident. Russ made an eerie prediction: he told Jo Lynn if anything should happen to him, Barbara was probably responsible.

Ten years earlier, Barbara's first husband, Larry Ford, had been shot in the head with a .25 caliber pistol, the same type of gun that killed Russ Stager. Barbara had told police that the gun went off as Larry Ford was cleaning it. Police were immediately suspicious, and the post-mortem investigation did nothing to allay their skepticism.

During the autopsy, Larry Ford's hands were checked for gunpowder residue, and none was found. This apparently proved that the death could not be suicide. If it was an accident, the only way Larry could have shot himself was by dropping the gun and causing it to discharge. But, because of the position of the gun and the shell casings homicide detectives rejected that theory.

A second autopsy was ordered, and the results clearly

showed that Larry had been shot at close range. This disproved the accident theory, and the death was reclassified from "accident" to "murder." But soon it was reclassified again. The local police department went through several changes of leadership and, unbelievably, the case went cold for lack of attention. After a few years it was officially ruled an accident, and Barbara received a $70,000 insurance settlement.

With her second husband dead under remarkably similar circumstances, authorities decided to take a close look at the couple's marriage. They found that Barbara and Russ had lived a lifestyle that went well beyond the means of a high school teacher. They had purchased a boat, new cars, a large home, exquisitely decorated interiors, and designer clothes.

On February 4, 1988, Sgt. Buchanan went to interview Barbara Stager, and wanted to do more than just ask questions. He thought Barbara's story of trying to pull the gun from under the pillow while her husband was sleeping made no sense at all, and thought that if he could get her to reenact what had happened he might get some unexpected information.

He came with two other homicide detectives: one would play Russ Stager in this "reenactment" and the other would videotape it. As Barbara attempted to demonstrate her version of events to police she apparently realizes—on-camera—that her story is inconsistent. She starts moving around on the bed in an attempt to make her story fit the facts of the "accident." The tape was damaging to Barbara, but she didn't seem to realize it. As the detectives were leaving the house, she asked him if they thought the investigation would close soon. She said she was waiting to file the insurance claim.

Local prosecutors were cautious as they built a case against Barbara Stager; they were convinced she'd gotten away with murder once and wanted to make sure it didn't happen again. Eugene Bishop, a firearms expert, did a series of tests on the pistol that killed Russ Stager. Bishop tried to determine if it would jam, if it were prone to accidental discharges, and in what direction it ejected shell casings.

He fired eight rounds from a magazine, and the pistol didn't jam. He beat it on a mat to see if it would discharge accidentally, and it didn't. Webster found that the safety on the pistol was unusually difficult to switch off. Barbara's contention that the safety "slipped" off when she pulled from under the pillow was inconsistent with all tests performed on the gun.

In addition, the shell casings in test firings ejected, with some force, to the right and rear of the shooter. The shell casing at the actual shooting was found at the head of the bed, between two pillows. If the gun had been fired from where Barbara Stager said it had—from bed level—the spent shell casing should have been found lower on the bed, or perhaps even on the floor. In any event, it would not have gone forward.

With enough probable cause to check the Stagers' financial records, investigators soon discovered the couple was deeply in debt, and it wasn't hard to figure out how. Numerous checks had been written from Russ's account—and signed in his name—to Barbara. But handwriting analysis later proved that the signature on the checks was not Russ's, and that the writing was actually consistent with Barbara's handwriting. Still, despite the forgeries, the couple simply did not have enough money to pay their debts and were facing bankruptcy.

Prosecutors now had a clear motive. If Russ died "accidentally" Barbara would stand to claim about $100,000 from insurance policies. The firearms analysis made it clear that her story was not consistent with the facts of the shooting. And she had another husband who died under similar circumstances, and from his death she received a large amount of insurance money. This was not likely to be admissible in court, but police were convinced they had a two-time murderer on their hands and brought Barbara to trial.

Just as the proceedings began, a startling piece of evidence surfaced. A student at Durham High School found an audio cassette tape under one of the bleachers. When he listened to it, he was shocked to hear Coach Stager's voice saying he feared for his life. On the tape, recorded just three days before his death, Russ Stager said he believed Barbara was trying to poison him with an overdose of drugs.

Here's part of the actual transcript: "The last few nights Barbara has woke [sic] me and gave me what she said was two aspirin. She stood there to see if I took it. I did not take it. Placed it under the bed." He goes on to say that a few nights before he actually took some medicine Barbara gave him and woke up with a debilitating headache and nausea.

Russ Stager also mentioned his suspicions about the death of Barbara's first husband: "The first one, I don't know what happened. But according to his parents, there was some foul play going on. He supposedly accidentally shot himself in their bedroom. I had no idea what really went on and what really happened. She was there when it happened. My question is, did her husband, Larry Ford, accidentally shoot himself? I'm just being paranoid about this stuff. Sometimes I wonder."

The defense claimed the tape was a fabrication. But forensic audio experts analyzed the voice and said their was no doubt: the voice was Russ Stager's, and the tape had not been altered. Prosecutors told jurors it was like having a "voice from the grave." And indeed it was—the victim predicted his own murder.

The jury deliberated for just forty-three minutes before finding Barbara Stager guilty. She was sentenced to life in prison.

This story is unusual for a lot of reasons, not least that there are two different attempts to "shoot the lie." The first is by the homicide investigators themselves and it is perhaps one of the most compelling pieces of video we've ever shown. Not because anything particularly violent happens—the video is nothing more than Barbara Stager playacting the shooting on a bed. But any objective observer can see that her story doesn't comport with the facts. She has to literally contort herself to try and make her version of the story work. And it's a strange thing to watch, not the least because she seems so completely unconcerned that she's being caught in a lie. Detective Buchanan, the homicide investigator who set up the reenactment, said later that it was as weird a thing as he'd seen in his entire career. "I was standing face-to-face with a killer," he told us. "I knew it, but she didn't know I knew it."

In the police version they don't spend a lot of time on Barbara pulling the gun out from under her husband's head. They were more interested in Barbara's position on the bed when the shooting happened. We, on the other hand, tried to re-create her entire story—getting up, slipping her hand under her husband's sleeping head, and trying to pull the gun from under the pillow. It is a preposterous story, and one made only more so by any attempt to re-create it. In take after take our actress tried to make this believable, but no matter how hard she tried it always looked like she was up to no good. The act of trying to pull a pistol from under the head of a sleeping person looks like a criminal act. And there's a good reason: the only reason someone would do something like that is to do something criminal. You watch the "lie" and can't stop asking the obvious question: why doesn't she just wake him up? The answer, of course, is that if he's awake he's harder to kill.

Homicide investigators on the case described Barbara Stager as a "textbook sociopath." By that they meant that she was so intent on getting what she wanted—killing her husband so she could get the insurance payment—that she never considered how ludicrous her story was, let alone the devastating consequences Russ's murder would have not only on his friends and family, but her two sons. Amazingly, she also never considered that the "accidental" death of her first husband would be reexamined. Incidentally, that case was never reopened. Since Barbara was clearly going to be in prison for life for the murder of her second husband, local authorities decided it wasn't worthwhile to reinvestigate the death of her first.

Also, if you get a chance to see this episode, make sure to check out the computer animation that shows the trajectory of the fatal bullet. The path of the bullet was one of many things that put the lie to Barbara's story. Investigators proved that Russ Stager was shot from a position on top of his body, not from bed-level, as Barbara claimed. The animation exactly matches the set we used to re-create the murder. There are sections in the episode where we intercut between the re-creation and the animation. This was the opposite of "shooting the lie." The effect is almost clinical—the juxtaposition of live actors and computer animated models performing what science proved actually happened in the Stager bedroom is chilling. Between the actors and the animation we see what really happened, and the premeditation on Barbara Stager's part becomes immediately apparent.

That premeditation becomes even more obvious when you hear Russ Stager's audiotape predicting his own murder. It was entered into evidence and therefore made available to us. We play almost all of it, and hearing it will make you sad and enraged by turns. He seemed sure the end was coming, but for some reason couldn't bring himself to just get up and leave.

FOUR
"It Wasn't Me"

While most of the cases featured on *Forensic Files* show how science leads to a conviction, we've done a number of cases where that same science sets innocent people free. For us, as for people in law enforcement, these stories are distressing. After seeing forensic technology used to overcome seemingly insurmountable obstacles and secure convictions, it is both harrowing and depressing to see that in some cases—admittedly rare—it's used to put an innocent person behind bars.

Take the case of Ray Krone, a case we called "Once Bitten."

Ray was a postman in Phoenix, Arizona; an Air Force veteran with no prior criminal record. He loved to play darts, and was involved in a number of competitive leagues. One of his favorite places to play was a small bar called The CBS Lounge in downtown Phoenix. He became friends with one of the bartenders, Kim Ancona, a divorced mother of three young children.

"It Wasn't Me"

One afternoon Ray got a knock on his front door. Two policemen asked him if he knew Kim Ancona. He said he did—that they were acquaintances from the CBS Lounge. The policemen then told him that Kim had been murdered that morning. Someone had come into the CBS Lounge after closing and had stabbed her to death in the men's bathroom. There was no sign of forced entry, and there were two drinks sitting on the bar, indicating to police that Kim had let her killer in—that she probably knew him.

The police asked Ray if he had set up a date with Kim for the previous night. He said, no, that he didn't know Kim well enough to date her. They said Kim told her coworkers they were dating. Ray said he had no idea why she would say such a thing.

Then police asked him to do something strange. They asked him if he'd be willing to bite down on a Styrofoam plate and Ray willingly complied. The next day he was arrested and charged with first-degree murder. Police said there was a bite mark on Kim Anona's left breast and that Ray's bite impression matched perfectly.

Ray had an alibi for the night in question, and was confident the killer would soon be found and he'd be set free. He was so confident he figured he'd save money by taking the public defender the state was willing to give him for free. But days, and then months went by, and the killer was not found. Ray remained behind bars, and soon stood trial.

He watched as prosecutors told jurors he was obsessed with Kim Ancona, that he was desperate for him to move in with her and that when she refused he flew into a rage and killed her. He watched as a highly respected forensic odontologist played a videotape that he said proved conclusively that it was Ray Krone's bite marks on Kim Ancona's chest. He watched as a jury found him guilty and sentenced him to death.

Numb, and broke, Ray Krone went to death row. His family

tried to scrape together enough money to mount an appeal. They found a defense lawyer named Christopher Plourd, a specialist in difficult forensic cases, who looked at the file and was outraged. He said Ray should never have been charged and pointed to a host of evidence that was ignored by prosecutors:

- A footprint from a size 9½ sneaker was found on the freshly cleaned floor of the CBS Lounge the night of the murder. Ray wore size 11 shoes.
- Foreign hairs were found on the body—Mongoloid hairs, meaning they came from someone of Asian or Native-American descent, certainly not from Ray Krone.
- Unidentified fingerprints in the bathroom where the murder happened were not Ray Krone's.
- And worst of all, Plourd said the bite mark evidence was among the worst he'd ever seen presented in court.

Plourd hired his own forensic odontologist, Dr. Norman "Skip" Sperber. He explained that skin is a notoriously difficult medium for retaining bite marks—it's soft, it moves when it's manipulated, and will expand or contract depending on how much moisture is present. Dr. Sperber had seen some clear bite marks in his career and graded them on a scale of 1 to 10 in terms of quality. He said the bite mark on Kim Ancona's chest did not even rate a "4" on that scale, and that even so, a detailed analysis showed the mark was not from Ray Krone. The measurements between the teeth simply did not match up.

Three years after his first conviction Ray Krone finally had his retrial. The forensic ondontologist who testified against him the first time repeated the same testimony. Dr. Sperber countered, saying the evidence clearly indicated someone other than Ray Krone had bitten Kim Ancona. Christopher

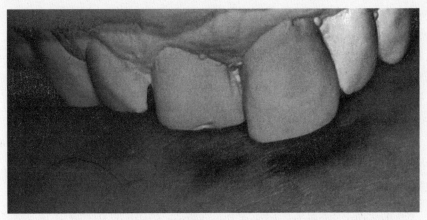

Evidence photo of Ray Krone's bite case being placed over the actual wound. Juries in two cases were fooled by this alleged match.

Plourd presented the rest of the case: the hairs that were not Ray's; the shoe prints that were not his; the fingerprints that belonged to someone else.

In what he later described as the most depressing moment of his life, Ray Krone was found guilty a second time. The judge in the case was so concerned about the verdict that he considered voiding the jury's decision. In the end he decided to let it stand, but would not allow the death penalty, saying there was an outside chance an innocent man would be executed.

Six more years went by. Then, Arizona became one of the first states to pass legislation allowing convicts access to post-conviction DNA testing. Chris Plourd went into action. When Kim Ancona was bitten the killer's teeth had gone through a tank top she was wearing. Saliva in that top was tested for DNA, and that DNA profile was put through a database of known offenders. Almost immediately there was a match. The DNA belonged to Kenneth Phillips, a native-American who, at the time of Kim Ancona's murder, lived just six hundred yards away from the CBS Lounge. Phillips was now approaching the end of a ten year sentence for child molestation.

Phillips's hair was compared to hairs found on Ancona's body: they were consistent. His fingerprints were compared to the unknown fingerprints found in the bathroom near the body: they were his. When confronted with the evidence, he told lawyers that on the night of Kim Ancona's murder he had an alcoholic blackout and woke up the next morning covered with blood. The evidence clearly indicated that Phillips was the murderer, even if he didn't remember it.

After ten years in prison Ray Krone walked out of prison a free man—the one hundredth convict to be released on the strength of DNA evidence. *Forensic Files* contacted the odontologist who helped put him behind bars. He didn't return our calls.

When we caught up with Ray Krone he had been out of prison for less than a year, and was working to adjust back to life in the "real world." In his backyard, half buried under the snow, was a giant piece of plywood with "Welcome Home, Ray" spray painted in gigantic letters of florescent orange. The colors had started to fade, and for Ray it seemed the novelty of being free was fading away as well. He was worried about what he was going to do next. And it was easy to see why. He'd certainly not acquired any job skills on death row.

For a man who had ten years of his life ripped away because of an overzealous prosecution, he was remarkably free of bitterness. He said he had nothing against the people who convicted him, but wanted to make sure some fail-safe was in place to make sure no one else got falsely convicted.

Ray was almost painfully shy. He often apologized for some perceived slight or breach of manners, saying he was still unsure of himself after so much time behind bars. The strange thing was that if we didn't know he'd spent time in prison it never would have occurred to us. He seemed to think, however, that it was obvious, as if he'd been branded with some sort of sign that said "Ex-con." It wasn't. He was a sweet-hearted, gentle guy, and no one could ever guess that hardships he'd endured.

Ray found some solace in traveling around the country lobbying for post-conviction DNA results being made available to anyone who requests them. He was also—no surprise—a staunch opponent of the death penalty, and missed no opportunity to rail against it. When our cameraman told him his wife supported the death penalty, Ray asked if there was a number where he could reach her. The cameraman said yes, dialed the number on his cell phone and handed it over. Ray proceeded to introduce himself and then politely told this total stranger that if Arizona justice had been just a little quicker he'd have been executed for a crime he didn't commit. Who knows whether that argument changed her mind, or anyone's, but you could clearly see that Ray Krone was going to make that argument as often as he could.

If you watch the "Once Bitten" episode you'll see video of Ray walking around a grocery store near his house. We had to ask the manager's permission to bring our cameras inside. The manager was already familiar with the story. Ray Krone finally returning home was big local news. The manager shook Ray's hand, gave him a gift certificate for $50, and welcomed him back. Ray, a bit embarrassed, thanked him. People knew his face and it was clear he was a bit uncomfortable with the attention.

While it's easy to blame prosecutors in situations like Ray Krone's, they're almost always acting in good faith. Ray's prosecutors were absolutely convinced he was guilty; they couldn't know they'd been misled by a forensic odontologist who privately expressed doubts about the validity of his own testimony.

There are, however, some cases where the desire for a guilty verdict gets the better of a prosecutor's judgment. A case in point is one we called "Man's Best Friend," a story so rife with tragedy we considered not doing it, in spite of some of the most interesting forensic science we've ever encountered.

Eager to raise their kids in a rural environment, John Miller and his common-law wife, Debbie Loveless, moved to a Texas farmhouse with five acres of land. In January 1989, John was clearing brush while Debbie was inside cleaning the house. Each thought their four-year-old daughter April was with the other, and panicked when they soon realized that April had spent most of the afternoon unsupervised.

They scoured the property, and eventually found her, face down and naked, with what appeared to be scratches and bruises all over her body. They rolled her over and found a large gash on her leg. John, a certified paramedic, administered first aid while Debbie called an ambulance. As John tried to stop the leg wound from bleeding he asked April what happened. He later testified that she said, "Dogs did it."

April died a few hours later. Her tiny body could not survive so much trauma.

A day later an autopsy was performed. The pathologist claimed there was nothing in April's wounds consistent with an animal attack. He said there was clear evidence that April was a battered child. Investigators went to John Miller's farm to see if there was any evidence there that supported the pathologist's findings. They found a broken electric curling iron, which the pathologist said could have been used to inflict the scratches on April's body. They found a knife John had just been given for Christmas.

They also found some books on witchcraft and the occult, which led them to theorize that April had been murdered as part of a Satanic ritual.

The knife and curling iron were tested for blood. The curling iron came back clean, but the knife was found to have two tiny spots that could not be conclusively identified as human blood.

This, however, was enough to arrest John Miller and Debbie Loveless. The pathologist said the fatal wound to April's leg was inflicted by a large, sharp object, and the knife appeared to be it.

Prosecutors, convinced that Miller and Loveless were guilty, did their best to get them to testify against each other. Plea bargains were offered and rejected. Only one defense exhibit was presented at trial. A chemist from the state crime lab testified that a thorough test on the Miller's knife indicated there was no blood on it. No testimony concerning a possible dog attack was ever heard by the jury.

Miller and Loveless were found guilty of first-degree murder and sentenced to life in prison. Shortly afterward, their appeal was rejected and it seemed clear they would spend the rest of their lives behind bars. They lost custody of their surviving child.

Luckily, a lawyer named Robert Ardis was familiar with the case and believed the couple had not received a fair trial. Ardis and his wife, Laura, a legal assistant, got hold of photos taken before and during the autopsy—photos that had not been made available to the original defense team. They saw what appeared to be a series of parallel lines on April's torso as well as what looked to be paw prints on her back. Perhaps, they thought, there was a reason the original defense had not been given access to these pictures.

The pictures were given to a new forensic pathologist, Dr. Charles Odom. He identified the four parallel lines as scratch marks from an animal, and confirmed that the prints on April's back were indeed paw prints—from a dog. He looked at photos taken of April's thigh wound before and after April came out of the emergency room. Suddenly it was clear why the original pathologist claimed the fatal wound was made with a sharp instrument: a surgical scalpel had made the incision while April was being treated in the emergency room. The original pathologist never saw the actual wound!

Four more forensic experts, armed with complete photographic evidence, supported this opinion.

After five long years in prison, during which they rarely saw their surviving daughter, the charges against John Miller and Debbie Lawless were dropped. But their marriage didn't survive the ordeal; they divorced shortly afterward.

Of all worst-case scenarios, this must surely rank near the top of the list: Finding your child just moments after she suffers fatal injuries; barely coping with the trauma when the authorities say they are absolutely certain that you are the one who inflicted those injuries; then ostracized by the community, by your friends, and even some members of your family. Then the state comes at you with everything they've got, and you barely have the resources to mount a credible, competent defense. You're paraded in public as a devil-worshipping child killer during a high-profile trial. Then you are found guilty and sent away for life. And the whole time you know you've done nothing wrong.

When we got to interview Debbie Loveless she'd been out of prison for more than five years but was still traumatized by what happened to her and to her daughter. Her account, even after all those years, is among the saddest, most harrowing interviews this program has ever done. In her own words, here is what it was like in the weeks after she was arrested:

"Just losing April was devastating. I didn't sleep for a long time after they arrested us because I could remember what she looked like before we had found her that day. And my mom sent me a picture, so that I could put it on the wall—because I couldn't close my eyes and see anything except for the way that she was when we found her—and the way she looked when she died."

To make matters worse, even Robert Ardis, Debbie's attorney, was concerned about the impartiality of the court and the prosecution's apparent unwillingness to consider alternate theories of April's death. He told the judge, who was not willing to have the court pay for a defense expert, that without some sort of alternative testimony he was convinced any eventual guilty verdict would be overturned on the grounds of "ineffective assistance to counsel." In other words, the deck was stacked against the defense. The judge dismissed Ardis's protests, but eventually an appeals court decided exactly that.

What is perhaps most disturbing about the case is that the evidence was available all along, and was plainly obvious to anyone who looked at it. The case is a textbook example of what happens when science is not allowed to play a role in a prosecution. Had proper science been introduced in this case, it's more than likely that Debbie Loveless and John Miller would never have been charged, let alone convicted. As it happened, a community made a decision about their guilt long before trial—a decision that was influenced by a prosecutor's zeal for a conviction even if the science didn't bear out the facts of his case. After all, a jury of one's peers can't be expected to render justice if key facts are withheld or distorted.

We'll give the last word on this one to Robert Ardis, the defense attorney who had taken it upon himself to make sure a court heard the true facts of the case: "It was five years out of their lives—done without any justification. I think it was a miscarriage of justice—oh, I think so. But I don't think I've ever done anything in my life that made me any happier. I can't speak for John and Debbie, but I'm sure they felt the same way."

Most likely they were just as happy as Robert Ardis. Still, their marriage didn't survive, and we're told there's virtually no contact between Debbie and John. They both moved far away from the town in which they were wrongfully convicted.

For Kevin Lee Green, the end of his marriage cost him sixteen years of his life for an attempted murder he had nothing to do with. Early in the evening of September 30, 1979, Green returned home to his Tustin, California, home to find his twenty-one-year-old wife, Dianna, unconscious. Nine months pregnant, she had been savagely raped and beaten. The news outraged the community and police were hard-pressed to deliver a suspect.

During the four weeks Dianna lingered in a coma, she gave birth to a stillborn baby girl named Chantel Marie. Dianna survived the attack but was left with memory loss, deafness in her left ear, and a speech impediment. She has never fully recovered and, in a development that had tragic consequences for her husband, she believes to this day that he was her attacker.

But in the immediate aftermath Dianna could not recall the attack, and the only significant evidence was the attacker's semen. This was 1979, before DNA was used in court, and investigators turned to blood-typing, the only means at their disposal.

The semen found at the scene was from a man described as a "secretor." About three quarters of the population will secrete blood cells into their semen and other bodily fluids, and this provided a crucial piece of evidence: the man who had raped Dianna Green had type-O blood. Kevin Green also had type-O blood.

Police interrogated Green. He told them that as he was returning home from a fast-food restaurant he saw a black man leaving his house in a van. Green told investigators he rushed into the house, found his wife unconscious and battered, and called police. He said his glimpse of the black man leaving his house was so brief he could not help in providing a composite sketch.

Months later, while still recuperating, Dianna was reading a baby magazine and claimed to have a flashback to the night of the attack. She remembered that before the attack, she and

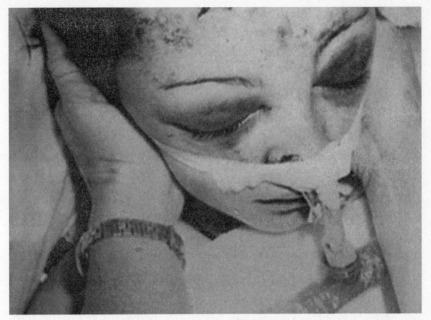

Evidence photo of Dianna Green. The blow was so forceful she never clearly remembered what happened to her.

Kevin had an argument. Kevin had wanted to have sex, but Dianna refused; she recalled that this made him angry. The next thing Dianna remembered was waking up from her coma in the hospital.

Such an episode of memory loss/recovery is called "traumatic amnesia," and stirs considerable controversy among psychologists. There have been instances when such recollections have proven to be true. There have been instances when they have no basis in fact.

Police, eager for a suspect, and convinced by the blood-typing tests and Dianna's recovered memory, were sure Kevin Green was their man. He was a Marine corporal, and they felt his military training could have given him a propensity for such violence. There were also rumors among friends and even family that he was not happy with the pregnancy and had no desire for children. In Kevin Green police had a suspect with motive and means, and they also had evidence, however tenuous, to link him to the crime.

Kevin Green was arrested and went to trial in November 1980. He was derided in the press as the worst sort of killer: a man who raped his wife and in the process killed his unborn child. He received no sympathy in the community, a situation which was not helped by prosecutors' well-publicized claims that they were sure they had their man.

The jury found Kevin Green guilty of the second-degree murder of his unborn daughter and the rape and assault of his wife. His sentence was fifteen-years-to-life.

While in prison, Kevin Green maintained his innocence. He stood by his story that he was out getting hamburgers when his wife was attacked. DNA testing was in its infancy, and Green simply couldn't afford the tests. He was fifteen years into his prison term before he was given the chance to prove his innocence.

In the early 1990s, The Orange County Sheriff's Office began establishing a DNA database, which keeps a record of offenders' DNA profiles. When there is an unsolved case, the DNA profile taken from a crime scene is cross-referenced with the DNA of known offenders in the state, often resulting in a match.

In 1995, staffers at the crime lab were updating their computer database with thousands of DNA "fingerprints" from state files. During this process they found a match between an incarcerated rapist's DNA and DNA found at the crime scenes of five murdered women in Orange County. This matching of DNA from two unrelated sources in the database is known as a "cold hit," and is rare.

The cold hit in question led them to Gerald Parker, a forty-one-year-old Marine who was in prison for the rape of a thirteen-year-old girl. Authorities now believed that Parker was the man known as the "Bedroom Basher." The Bedroom Basher attacked, raped, and bludgeoned five women in their homes in Orange County between 1978 and 1979. Tests on DNA recovered at these scenes subsequently proved Parker was the perpetrator.

Knowing that he could not dispute the DNA findings, Parker confessed to the crimes. Then he told investigators that he had to make one more confession. He said he was responsible for the rape of Dianna Green and the murder of Chantel Marie Green. Parker was able to present details of the crime scene "right down to the color of the lampshades in the house," according to investigators.

It is not uncommon for people facing life in prison to confess to crimes they did not commit. Authorities were also reluctant to consider the possibility that Kevin Green might have spent more than fifteen years behind bars for a crime committed by another man. But now there was proof—scientific proof. Forensic technology would now be able to tell investigators who had raped Dianna Green and killed her unborn daughter. They went back to the evidence file to retrieve the semen sample taken from crime scene in 1979.

Because the sample had been degraded over time the standard RFLP test was inadequate. Analysts instead turned to PRC testing. A PCR test takes a small sample, extracts any remnant of its nucleic DNA, and essentially photocopies it until there is enough to obtain a genetic profile. PCR is not as refined as RFLP, but in instances where there is little genetic material it is the best, and sometimes only, alternative.

In this case, the DNA from Gerald Parker matched the genetic fingerprint taken from the sixteen-year-old semen swab—proof that it was Gerald Parker and not Kevin Green who was responsible for the rape of Dianna Green.

Kevin Green was freed immediately. He had spent sixteen

years in prison for a crime he did not commit. He got a mere ten-thousand-dollar restitution from the state. Gerald Parker was sentenced to death.

Any viewer of *Forensic Files* who has seen this episode, which we entitled "Memories," has seen the interrogation video of Gerald Parker. His story is among the strangest we've ever heard, and his comments to police—all on videotape—are bone-chilling.

Parker was shy—so shy he had never had a romantic relationship with a woman. Yet he still desired sex, and this made for a tragically lethal combination. The only way Parker could manage to approach a woman was to beat her unconscious. Once she was incapacitated he was able to have sex—hence, his nickname, "The Bedroom Basher."

In the interrogation tape Parker gives a graphic description of how he assaulted Dianna Green. He describes what happened and then gets quiet as he approaches the actual assault. At the point where he strikes Dianna Green he repeatedly brings both hands down on the table and smacks it with such force that even hardened detectives in the room seem surprised. Parker, on the other hand, seems completely unfazed, as if he were talking about picking up a quart of milk at the local grocery store.

His actions on the tape created a dramatic opportunity for us to tell this particular story. In our re-creation the actor playing Parker enters Dianna's bedroom and then raises his hand to strike. An enterprising videotape editor decided to use this moment to cut to the actual interrogation tape—something we'd never done before. The juxtaposition of our actor re-creating what happened and Parker re-creating the actual event for police was eerie.

When the producers were called into the room to pronounce judgment on whether this particular "cut" was effective, the verdict was unanimous. All of us were surprised by how well the sequence worked. It's one of the strange things about television; things happen that you can't possibly anticipate, and they are often better for not having been planned.

This story created a number of problems for producers, both in the field and in the edit suite. For some time police did not know who the attacker was. When they finally settled on a suspect, they chose the wrong man. The dilemma for us was how to tell the story in a coherent way without buying into— in effect confirming—the mistakes made by police. We needed to film the attacker in a way that would convey the violence of what happened while keeping him completely anonymous. The fact that the wrongly convicted person was white and the actual attacker African-American only compounded the problem. If viewers were able to identify the race of the attacker we, as producers, would be indicating that we knew how the story ended *before* it actually ended. Granted, we do have the benefit of hindsight when we do these stories, but our intention is to let the evidence lead us—and the viewers—to the conclusion.

So the question was how to show the attack but keep the attacker anonymous. The solution was to shoot one of our actors with extreme backlighting—in effect silhouetting him against a wave of light. In the edit room this image was essentially cut out and then laid over itself numerous times. The final effect was a menacing figure shimmering in a sort of glowing half-light. The attacker can be identified as a man and nothing else. If you watch this particular episode you can't mistake the image.

As for Kevin Green, let's let him speak for himself. Here's what he said when we asked him what it was like during his first months prison:

"It is a mean place to be. This was reality. I could not live in a fantasy [that] one day this will all get worked out and then— as I saw what happened around me to other people, to my case, to my family, I got mad. I got angry. I got thrown in a hole because five guys wanted to kill me because I was in prison for the death of a baby."

After ten years in prison, Kevin told us, he'd become resigned that he'd never get out. He said that once he gave up hope of being released it became easier to adjust to life behind bars. Imagine having to make that kind of decision. And then imagine what it was like when the authorities finally told him they'd unearthed evidence of what he'd been telling them all along: that someone else, someone who fit the exact description he had given them, was the actual attacker.

Again, let's let Kevin tell us his story. Here's a quote, one which ended up being cut from our program, in which he describes the day he was told he'd be leaving prison: "They told me to keep it quiet, but the word went out like wildfire. I had corrections officers calling from home, calling in to say goodbye, congratulations. Can't believe that you, you've done all this time. My God. Inmates coming out of, out of the woodwork, you know, out, out of cells to come and say goodbye as I went up the hallway. You know, it's like instead of running a gauntlet I was, you know—if we had ticker tape, I'd have had a parade. It was great. And they kept explaining that if this had to happen to anybody, this kind of a release, they were just so glad it happened to me instead of maybe somebody that had done their time bitterly and angrily and, and hurt other people and things, you know—that they were happy for me. And we left the prison."

When we last caught up with Kevin, he was working at a California Wal-Mart, thrilled to be free, and with no apparent regrets about the sixteen years that had been taken away from him. Even though his wife's testimony helped land him in jail, he was protective of her, asking that we limit our contact with her and her family. After all, he told us, "she's more of a victim in this thing than I am."

"It Wasn't Me"

From our re-creation. The "Blurry Man" shot. How do you re-create a mistaken "memory?"

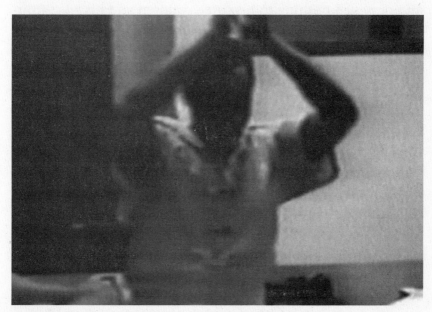

A still from police interrogation video. Gerald Parker shows how he struck the nearly fatal blow.

Strangely, in all of the cases in this chapter, there are people who, despite the evidence, still think the wrong person did it. But DNA and other forensic evidence doesn't lie—or perhaps it does, if it's manipulated or key parts of it are ignored. Take, for example, a case we called "Dessert Served Cold."

Shortly after 10 P.M. on January 21, 1990, sixty-one-year-old Richard M. Alfredo sat down to a late-night snack of lime Jell-O at his home near New Bedford, Massachusetts. An hour later Christina Martin, his thirty-nine-year-old live-in companion of five years, frantically called 911. She said Alfredo was having trouble breathing, and was complaining of chest pains. He was rushed to a nearby hospital where he died two hours later of what was officially listed as a massive heart attack. Since there was apparently nothing suspicious about the death, no autopsy was performed and Mr. Alfredo was buried three days later.

Mr. Alfredo left all of his modest estate to Christina Martin, and provided nothing to his three children and his wife, from whom he had been separated for eight years. His wife contested the will.

None of this was of any interest to New Bedford police until an informant told them that in the weeks prior to Mr. Alfredo's death Christina Martin and her fourteen-year-old daughter, Teasha Pauline, had been soliciting someone to help them kill him. Other informants—mostly high school friends of Teasha—backed up this story, but when confronted Ms. Martin denied there was involvement in Mr. Alfredo's death. Within days, however, she and her daughter had left the area, and provided no contact information.

Mr. Alfredo's wife and family became increasingly convinced that there was foul play, and five weeks after he was buried New Bedford police exhumed his body. Evidence was taken from various parts of Mr. Alfredo's corpse, including his fingernails and hair, and these were subjected to a test known as a Radio Immunoassay or RIA. This involves sending radio waves through biological samples that have been reduced to a liquid state. The waves measure concentrations of proteins or antibodies that have been produced by disease or infection.

Analysts found what they described as "massive amounts" of lysergic acid, or LSD, in Richard Alfredo's body. The drug is an extraordinarily powerful hallucinogen, discovered accidentally by a Swedish scientist in the 1930s. Though there are no known cases of anyone overdosing on LSD, the hallucinations it produces could be terrifying for someone who does not know if he or she is under its influence. The drug is tasteless, and easy to conceal and administer. A single drop can affect the user for up to twelve hours.

Police speculated that the hallucinations caused Mr. Alfredo to panic, and that this resulted in his fatal heart attack. Since some types of LSD are often "cut" with methamphetamine or other stimulants, there was a theory that this may also have contributed to Mr. Alfredo's death. Some of Teasha's high school friends also told police that she had bragged about killing her father "with Jell-O." This made some sense, at least in theory. Jell-O, because it's cold and sealed to the air, is an ideal way to conceal LSD. But by the time police came up with this theory the Jell-O had been disposed of, so there was no way to test it.

Soon, more informants came forward. A local drug dealer told police that Christina Martin and her daughter had bought a large amount of LSD the day before Mr. Alfredo's death. Warrants were issued for their arrests, but their whereabouts were still unknown.

A check of all rental car agencies, airlines, trains, and other transportation services indicated that Ms. Martin and her daughter had taken a train to Montreal just two days after being questioned by police. She was arrested by Canadian officials as she arrived at the restaurant where she worked as a waitress, and was then turned over to U.S. authorities. She had gone to some lengths to change her appearance: her hair had been cut short and dyed black.

Christina Martin pleaded not guilty to charges of first-degree murder and conspiracy. Her daughter Teasha was listed as an unindicted co-conspirator.

Prosecutors brought forward a parade of witnesses. Some testified that Ms. Martin tried repeatedly to hire a killer and failed. The drug dealer who sold her the LSD said it was clear she had no experience with the drug and that he was convinced she had no intention of using it herself. But the most damning testimony came from toxicologists testifying for the prosecution.

They said that Mr. Alfredo had no history of recreational drug use and that the amounts found in his body would be unusually high even for an experienced drug user. The theory that resulted was that Mr. Alfredo had not purposely ingested the LSD, and that Christina Martin had given him a massive dose because she intended to kill him. On one point they were clear: the LSD had caused Mr. Alfredo's death.

Ms. Martin's lawyers showed that Richard Alfredo had history of heart disease, was a heavy smoker, and had undergone a double-bypass operation fifteen years before his death—indicators, they said, that he had died of natural causes. They contested the toxicology evidence, but brought forward no expert witnesses. Even worse, the evidence that Mr. Alfredo had a history of heart disease bolstered the prosecution's argument, making it seem even more likely that Christina Martin was trying to induce a fatal heart attack.

After a three-week trial Christina Martin was found guilty of first-degree murder and sentenced to life in prison without parole. But the story doesn't stop there.

Eight years later Ms. Martin picked up some new legal representation, courtesy of the Committee for Public Counsel Services, an organization that provides legal help to people they believe have been wrongly convicted. The Committee was convinced that Ms. Martin's original lawyer failed to adequately contest the toxicology reports that ultimately convicted her.

They brought in a string of noted toxicologists, all of whom criticized the Radio Immunoassay test as inadequate and in need of verification. The RIA test is similar to what athletes are given in international competition. It's a screening test designed to be confirmed by a more refined method. On many occasions athletes have tested positive in the initial screening, only for medical authorities to find out later that the screening test was inaccurate.

In this case defense toxicologists testified that the embalming fluid found in the body was capable of giving off a reading that could be misinterpreted as LSD. They also found that the state did not disclose the results of the more refined test—a gas chromatograph/mass spectrometry test that showed no sign whatsoever of LSD in Mr. Alfredo's body. Gas Chromatography is considered the gold standard for detecting foreign substances in the body. It's a machine that breaks down the test sample to its fundamental molecular components. Its results are rarely, if ever, contested.

But most significantly, Christina Martin's new defense team pointed out that no one in medical history had ever died from ingesting LSD. There was no account of such a death anywhere in the world, even though toxicologists in the Ms. Martin's trial were clear that it was LSD that put Richard Alfredo in his grave.

Upon receiving this information a Superior Court judge threw out the conviction and ordered a new trial.

Before the second trial began, in August 1997, Christina Martin pleaded guilty to manslaughter. She continued to maintain her innocence, but decided to plead guilty when it became clear that competing toxicologists would contest the LSD evidence, and that her alleged attempts to solicit murder, as well as her fleeing the country after Mr. Alfredo's death, made it highly possible that she would again be convicted of first-degree murder and would spend the rest of her life behind bars. She was released for time served on the original conviction.

So, what do you think? Did she or didn't she? If you're unsure, you're not alone. Prosecutors remain convinced of her guilt, and so do a lot of people in New Bedford. Her lawyer says she was the victim of overzealous prosecutors and that the science proves it.

For many, her guilt or innocence remains an open question. Still, the fact remains that the best testing method available showed there was no LSD in Mr. Alfredo's system. Ms. Martin may have wanted him dead, may have talked about it, may have actually tried to make it happen, but the case against her was built on faulty science.

It's not an uncommon occurrence, and when it happens the jury—at least the jury of public opinion—remains out, sometimes indefinitely. Take one of the most infamous cases in Texas, a state known for infamous cases. We called it "Where the Blood Drops."

On September 16, 1987, Bill Mowbray was found dead in the bedroom of his home in Brownsville, just 150 miles from the Mexican border. The forty-three-year-old car dealer was the apparent victim of a self-inflicted gunshot wound. When paramedics arrived, Bill's wife, Susie Mowbray, told them she was asleep next to him when she heard him moving. She turned in his direction, and saw his elbow pointing up in the air. Seconds later she heard a loud explosion—the gunshot. She jumped out of bed, saw her husband bleeding with a gun at his side, moved the gun away and dropped it on the floor. She ran downstairs and made a call.

But it wasn't to 911. The first person she called was one of her husband's coworkers. She told him that what she'd feared for weeks had finally come to pass: Bill had killed himself. Then she called 911. When police and paramedics arrived they were greeted by a calm Susie Mowbray, so calm, in fact, that she met them with a drink in one hand and a cigarette in the other.

Bill Mowbray was found in a sleeping position—with the covers pulled up all the way to his neck. The fatal wound was a contact wound. The gun barrel had been placed directly against Bill's head. As the bullet exited his left temple it went through his left hand, which was apparently resting under his head when the gun was fired. This meant he had to have used his right hand to fire the gun. But that hand was under a blanket, and had no trace of blood on it.

This was strange. The weapon was a .357 magnum, a big gun that, in the case of a contact wound, would have created large amounts of what is known as "blowback." When a gun of that size is fired at close range, blood and brain matter blow back on to the hand of the shooter.

Susie and Bill were the only people in the room. Even Susie claimed no one else was there. So the fatal shot had to come from one of two people: Susie or her husband. For Susie Mowbray's story to be plausible it would mean her husband got up, pulled the gun from the nightstand, went back and lay down in bed, shot himself and then, inexplicably, pulled up the covers after he'd been shot at point-blank range.

When asked why her husband would commit suicide she said the car business was in trouble and that their debts were mounting. She described Bill as distraught, and said that in the last weeks he'd grown increasingly frantic with worry. Within hours of the shooting she invited friends over. They pulled up the bedroom carpets and painted the room. Some people— including Bill's family—thought this behavior was downright bizarre; others said that getting the room cleaned up and erasing all traces of the suicide made perfect sense.

For police, it was time to take a closer look at Susie. Many people in Brownsville had little trouble believing that she was capable of killing Bill. Susie Mowbray was known as something of a spoiled debutante, whose taste for the finer things far exceeded the income of her struggling car-dealer husband. She stood to get almost two million dollars in life insurance upon Bill's death. When the insurance agent told police that Susie had come in to verify the details of the policy the day before Bill's death, even her supporters had to admit that things didn't look particularly good.

Less than three months after the shooting, Susie Mowbray was charged with Bill's murder. The trial began in June 1988, and the case hinged mainly on the testimony of blood-spatter expert, Sgt. Dusty Hesskew. He told jurors that he treated Susie's nightgown with Luminol and found 48 separate blood spatters. He claimed this blood was high-velocity blood spatter, which is a residual blood spatter that occurs when someone is shot at close range. He claimed this spatter would not be found on Susie's nightgown unless she was standing above her husband, not lying next to him as she had claimed.

Prosecutors reiterated the fact that Susie was the only other person in the room and the evidence clearly indicated that for Bill to have shot himself was physically impossible. They portrayed Susie as money-hungry and ruthless, saying that she was more than capable of cold-blooded murder if it would keep her living in the style to which she'd become accustomed.

After a three-week trial, Susie Mowbray was found guilty of first-degree murder and sentenced to life in prison.

Susie maintained her innocence and attempted three times to appeal her conviction, all to no avail. It was not until 1995 that Susie's case would make a complete turnaround.

Susie's son, Wade Burnett, was so outraged by his mother's dilemma that he enrolled in law school at Louisiana State University. He researched every aspect of the case, and soon concluded that his mother had been wrongfully convicted.

Wade learned that blood evidence, which could have exonerated his mother, was withheld during the original trial. The prosecution had hired world-renowned blood expert, Herbert MacDonell, to test Susie Mowbray's nightgown for the presence of blood spatter. MacDonell had found no presence of blood on Susie's nightgown, which would have proven that Susie could not have fired the gun. The prosecution decided to ignore these findings, and hired another blood expert who would corroborate their theories.

But how did MacDonell account for another expert reaching the exact opposite conclusion? He said that some substances, such as bleach and even horseradish, will glow when in contact with Luminol. This creates a "false positive" that can easily be mistaken for blood. No confirmatory tests were ever conducted to see if the spatters on Susie's nightgown were blood . . . or something else.

Armed with this information, Wade Burnett filed a motion for a new appeal. The appeal was granted after a state district judge heard the new evidence and believed the original conviction should be ruled out under "Fundamental Fairness." On May 16, 1997, Susie Mowbray was released on a $35,000 bond, and eight months later, her new trial began.

The prosecution had to explain why, if Susie had shot her husband at point-blank range, there was no evidence of blood on her clothing. They theorized that she might have been lying next to Bill and had used a barrier of sheets and pillows to shield herself from the blood. But most of those blankets, and the T-shirt Bill was wearing when he died, had been lost in the eight years since the shooting. This was a devastating blow to the prosecution, but not nearly as devastating as their having to admit that they had withheld testimony during the first trial.

After a brief four-hour deliberation, the jury set Susie Mowbray free. But the verdict didn't put the case to rest. Even the jury seemed unsure about what happened. Minutes after the verdict, the jury foreman made this statement to the media:

"Members of the jury have reached the conclusion that the only issue decided by this jury is that the prosecution was unable to prove beyond a reasonable doubt the guilt of the defendant."

The outstanding questions still remain: If Bill Mowbray shot himself, how did he avoid getting any blood on his hands, and how did he manage to pull the covers over himself after suffering a fatal bullet wound? Even the experts are undecided. Here are two quotes that we ran back-to-back near the end of our program on the case.

From Lawrence Dahm, MD, Forensic Pathologist: "I can't be absolutely sure in a mathematical sense that she is the one who did it, but I am sure he did not shoot himself."

From Jim Shaw, Defense Lawyer: "It was a physical impossibility for her to have killed her husband."

If you've seen this particular episode you've seen one of the strangest courtroom displays in recent memory, a display that many believe almost sent Susie Mowbray back to jail. The prosecutor was in the middle of his closing argument: "She's smoking a cigarette, she's standing outside with a drink in her hand, she's medicating herself. He is still alive, drowning in his own blood!"

At this point—in the middle of the prosecutor's summation—Susie Mowbray jumps out of her seat and screams: "I didn't do it! Please! Don't let them do this to me again! I didn't do it! I love him!"

It may be an overstatement but this could come under the "must-be-seen-to-be-believed" category. Susie is literally hysterical and almost everyone in the courtroom stands up so as not to miss any of the outburst. When she's finished she collapses in a heap into the arms of her attorney, and the judge immediately clears the room.

The question became, was this a premeditated outburst, and would it prejudice the jury. The judge decided to let the case move forward and, interestingly, it was the defense that was most worried. They thought the jury might view Susie's outburst as a "grandstand play" and hold it against her. In the end, however, the simple fact that some evidence had been lost and some mishandled was apparently enough to establish reasonable doubt.

Another interesting sidebar on this story concerns blood spatter expert, Herbert MacDonell. In a small lab in Corning, New York, Mr. MacDonell has spent hours studying blood, how it travels, what it does on impact, how it's affected by temperature and virtually anything else you could think of. He wants prosecutors, investigators and defense attorneys to know as much as possible about blood and how it reacts to violence. To that end he holds symposiums in Corning and around the country for all levels of law enforcement. For him, correctly "reading" blood spatter provides the ultimate template to view a violent crime scene. If anyone were doubtful about his passion for his work, one look at his business card would put those doubts to rest: on a white background his name is emblazoned over what appears to be a giant spatter of blood. He's a wonderful guy, and we've enjoyed dealing with him on numerous cases.

Those who watched the O.J. Simpson trial might be familiar with Mr. MacDonell. He testified for the defense, and to this day maintains that the blood at the scene does not implicate O.J. Needless to say, the case aroused considerable passions, and many people who disagree with the verdict are therefore suspect of Mr. MacDonell. This held true with one of our producers, who interviewed Mr. MacDonell for a case far removed from O.J. Simpson's. Our producer, who was familiar with the details of the Simpson case and, because of her job, knew more about forensic science than the average layperson, was passionate in her belief that O.J. was guilty. She could recite her reading of the evidence practically chapter and verse, and for her Mr. MacDonell's testimony simply didn't hold water.

Passion is a good thing, and we were all happy that she was passionate about the Simpson case. But we were going to interview Mr. MacDonell for something completely unrelated, so senior management of *Forensic Files* made it clear to this producer that under no circumstances was she to initiate a conversation about the Simpson case. We knew that, once initiated, it was likely such a discussion would escalate into an argument. Since Mr. MacDonell was kind enough to give us his time we saw no need to antagonize him. The producer agreed and promised us that even if the Simpson case came up she would do her best to steer the conversation elsewhere.

We probably don't need to tell you what happened next. In the middle of the interview—on the unrelated case—our producer began to challenge Mr. MacDonell about his O.J. testimony. As she grew more heated and passionate, he became more calm and collected, repeating over and over that the evidence compelled him to testify in O.J.'s defense. Our producer grew increasingly frustrated—perhaps she was hoping he'd have some revelation in the middle of the interview and simply do an about-face on his testimony—until, finally, her professionalism got the better of her and she got down to the business at hand.

When *Forensic Files* management viewed the tape we of course saw the exchange—about three minutes long and initiated by our producer. After copious apologies on her part, we called Mr. MacDonell to smooth over any feathers that might have been ruffled in the "discussion." All he did was laugh and say that he had had that conversation so often he couldn't distinguish one altercation from the next. And then he told us about another case he thought we might be interested in, a case so unlikely we thought at first that he was joking (it wouldn't have been the first time). The case ultimately hinged on something Mr. MacDonell saw when he went to a local high school's production of *Peter Pan*.

We called the story "Accident or Murder."

When Clayton Johnson, a Nova Scotia schoolteacher, left for work on the morning of February 20, 1989, all appeared normal at his small suburban home. Within hours, his wife Janice was found dead and Mr. Johnson's life would be changed forever.

At 7:40 A.M., the school bus arrived to pick up the Johnson children. Next-door-neighbor Clare Thompson watched the children get on board and then called Janice Johnson for a chat. She later told police they talked for about ten minutes. They were briefly interrupted when Janice called to say goodbye to Clayton as he went to work. The phone call ended at about 7:50. Clayton was seen by acquaintances and a gas station attendant at various points during his twenty-mile drive to work.

At 7:51, the Johnson's other neighbor, a Mrs. Molloy, arrived to drop off her child at the Johnson home. She found Janice Johnson lying at the bottom of the basement stairs in a pool of blood. Janice died four hours later of massive blunt trauma to the head. Police initially believed that Johnson died as a result of an accidental fall. Two women from the Johnson's church went to the house and cleaned up the pool of blood after the body had been removed.

Nova Scotia's chief coroner had little trouble ruling the death an accident. He said that Mrs. Johnson had fallen forward down the stairs and that her head had wedged briefly in a five-and-one-half inch gap between the stairs and the wall. He said that flipped her over and landed her at the bottom of the stairs with massive contusions to her scalp.

Three months later, Clayton Johnson began dating a twenty-two-year-old member of his Pentecostal congregation, and they married within the year. When homicide investigator Brian Oldford heard this, he became suspicious and decided to reinvestigate. He learned that Clayton had taken out a $125,000 life insurance policy on Janice shortly before she died.

In addition, Brian Oldford interviewed the two women who had cleaned up the blood in the Johnson's basement after Janice Johnson was found. In their original statements, they made no reference to blood spatter anywhere else in the basement. After Sgt. Oldford showed them photos of the body, they changed their story. Though none of the EMTs or other personnel remembered seeing any other blood, the two women insisted they had seen not only a pool of blood, but spatters on the wall by the steps. This indicated to Sgt. Oldford that a fight had taken place before Mrs. Johnson went down the stairs. He found a piece of firewood that he thought might be the murder weapon, despite the fact that there was no evidence to that effect. In light of Oldford's theory, the coroner also changed his stance and said he thought Janice Johnson had been murdered.

There were no other suspects, and it appeared Clayton Johnson had motive. Prosecutors said he had designs on the young woman he eventually married and he also stood to gain financially by his wife's death. Clayton Johnson was charged with first-degree murder, found guilty, and sentenced to life in prison on May 4, 1993. The case against him was largely circumstantial, but higher courts refused to grant him an appeal.

His case caught the attention of lawyer James Lockyer of the Association in Defense of the Wrongfully Convicted. To him the case against Clayton Johnson did not bear scrutiny, and he began to dismantle it piece-by-piece.

• Lockyer did not believe that Johnson began the alleged "affair" with the younger woman before his first wife's death.

The town in which Clayton lived was so small it could not have gone unnoticed had it been going on before Janice died.

• He thought the prosecution hadn't proved that money was a motive. Locker found that the insurance policy on Janice Johnson was standard-issue for all teachers in the school district in which Clayton worked. It was optional but Clayton was among forty percent of the teachers who took advantage of it.

• As for the blood spatter, there was no evidence, except the dubious testimony of the two women, that it even existed. Even the judge in the case admitted that IF the blood spatter existed, it could have been caused by EMTs going about their work. There were also no wood fragments in Mrs. Johnson's head wounds, despite the fact that the alleged murder weapon was a piece of firewood; in fact, no murder weapon was ever found.

• As for the timing, numerous people had seen Mr. Johnson that morning at the same time the murder allegedly happened. Even if he did it, he would have had about ten minutes to beat his wife to death, clean the blood from his clothes and get to work. The timeline for the murder did not hold up.

The Canadian higher courts still refused to reopen the case. Mr. Lockyer, realizing he only had one chance to make his case, brought in two forensic experts: pathologist, Dr. Linda Norton, and blood-spatter specialist Herb MacDonell. Both believed that the biggest mistake the coroner made in his ruling was that Mrs. Johnson had fallen forward down the stairs. By examining the photos and nature of the injuries, they were convinced that she had fallen backward. The physical evidence, they insisted, would make sense if viewed from this perspective, particularly the head wounds and a long, linear bruise on the back of her left calf.

There was one problem. No one would listen. Mr. Mac-Donell was searching for a way to prove the "backward fall" theory to a jury when he attended a local high school play of *Peter Pan*. In it, he saw one of the actresses fly across the stage in a transom harness attached to her back and waist. After the play, he approached the young actress, Heather Murphy, and found she was exactly the same height and weight as Janice Johnson.

In one of the most unusual forensic demonstrations in the history of law enforcement, MacDonell then built an exact mock-up of the stairs on which Mrs. Johnson died, including the five- and-a-half-inch gap in which her head was allegedly caught, and he asked Heather to bring her transom harness for a series of experiments. These experiments were conducted on videotape.

Blue chalk powder was put on the side of the steps to mark Heather Murphy's head at any point she had contact. After some practice runs she was able to fall down the steps in the way that Mr. MacDonell claimed had resulted in Janice Johnson's death. The blue marks on Heather Murphy's head were a perfect match to the wounds found on Janice Johnson's head. The backward fall explained how Mrs. Johnson would have injured the top of her head (which the prosecution claimed was from a blow) and would also account for hair that was discovered in the gap in the steps.

The accidental backward-fall scenario would also account for the complete lack of defensive wounds on both Clayton Johnson and his wife—if they'd had the fight claimed by the prosecution it was more than likely that both of them would have sustained injuries on their arms, their hands, or both. Furthermore, Janice Johnson was alive when she was found by her neighbor. If Clayton had meant to kill her it seemed unlikely he would leave the house while she was still alive and able to identify him as her attacker.

When the full case was finally heard Canadian prosecutors released Clayton Johnson from prison, after he'd spent nearly six years behind bars. Two years later he was completely exonerated, but his marriage fell apart and he had to endure a long process of getting re-acquainted with his two school-age daughters. He's tried to resume his life, but as in most exoneration cases, there are people in his community who believe to this day that he killed his wife. The facts say clearly that he did not.

If you ever catch this episode, look carefully for the part where we re-create the "backward fall" theory. Getting an actress to appear as if she's falling backward down a flight of steps—without breaking her neck—was something you can plan for but never really anticipate. We ended up having the cameraman run under the steps while he twirled the camera in circles, catching light as it came through the slats between each step. As he did this the actress slid down as quickly as she could, supporting herself with the wall and the banister. It's surprisingly effective. And later in the program is a detailed computer animation of exactly how the backward fall happened. It proves the old dictum, "a picture speaks a thousand words." Forensic experts could explain this theory time and again, but the animation brings it home in a way that words never could.

FIVE
The Great Pretenders

Good guys—and women—gone bad. Even we are surprised how at many stories like this we've done. You might think that a fair percentage of the two-hundred cases we've covered would be about habitual offenders, hit men, and low-life criminals who finally got their comeuppance. In fact, the opposite is true.

A lot of the really interesting forensic stories don't often involve incorrigible bad guys. They involve people, who for whatever reason—money, lust, love, or long-hidden sociopathic tendencies—finally decide to commit a crime. These are the types who think things through, the types who think they're going to get away with it. To their neighbors, coworkers, and even their family, they present the picture of normalcy. But their murders are often more heinous for having been so meticulously planned. These are the people—we've all seen this clip on the local news at one time or another—whose astonished neighbors will tell a reporter: "He seemed like such a wonderful man. I just can't believe he'd be capable of something like this!"

We call them The Great Pretenders. And one of the greatest was featured in an episode we entitled "Past Lives."

Madison Rutherford was living the American dream. The thirty-four-year-old financial analyst was happily married and wanted for nothing. He and his wife Rhynie (pronounced "Rennie") lived in a beautiful upscale home in rural Connecticut, just a short drive from New York City.

Madison's success provided a sizeable amount of disposable income, and one of the ways the couple liked to dispose of it was buying rare dogs. In the summer of 1998, Madison and a friend drove south to Mexico to buy a Brazilian mastiff, a large dog distantly related to the pit bull.

A few days after Madison crossed the border, Mexican officials came upon a burned-out car near the industrial city of Monterrey. The driver of the car was still in the vehicle and burnt beyond recognition. In fact, the body was so damaged that local medical officials could not determine exactly how the driver died. He might have had a heart attack that caused the accident or he might have burned to death after the vehicle crashed. The official death certificate issued at the scene by Mexican authorities indicated the driver had been "totally carbonized," meaning the remains had all but disintegrated.

The task was now to identify the driver. Inside the car Mexican authorities found a wrist bracelet with the inscription "to Madison, Love Rhynie," as well as a MedicAlert pendant that signified the wearer was allergic to penicillin. For some reason both of these items had survived the fire relatively intact. Local officials ran the license plate on the vehicle and found it was rented to a "Madison Rutherford." The rental agreement listed the hotel where Rutherford was staying. His traveling companion was still there and confirmed that Rutherford was driving to Monterrey to pick up a dog, and that he always wore a MedicAlert pendant for a penicillin allergy.

This was enough for Mexican officials to establish identification. They identified the victim of the crash as Madison Rutherford, and ruled his death an accident. His wife was informed and called friends to her house to share her grief. One of these friends was Brigitte Beck, a native of Germany and naturalized U.S. citizen who had become close to the Rutherfords—so close that she had signed over power of attorney to Madison and gave him complete control of her finances.

Brigitte was grief-stricken, and worried. She was in her seventies and was unsure what would happen to her life savings now that Madison was dead. Her fears were not eased when, shortly after she arrived at the Rutherford's house, Rhynie pulled her aside and whispered in her ear that Madison is not dead.

Brigitte was shocked and asked where Madison was. Rhynie said she was unsure but was convinced her husband had not died, and that she would give Brigitte more information as soon as she heard from Madison.

In the meantime Rhynie submitted two separate claims for life insurance payments—totaling seven million dollars. This was a large payout, considerably more than might be expected, even from someone with Madison's income. He was wealthy, but not that wealthy, so the insurance companies decided to look into the circumstances of his death.

They didn't like what they saw. Their questions centered around how the inscribed bracelet and MedicAlert pendant had survived the fire when the body had been burned to ashes. Also, Rutherford was supposed to be transporting a dog, but no dog remains were found in the vehicle. When the vehicle was last seen there was a bicycle attached to the back bumper, but nothing resembling a bike was found at the crash site.

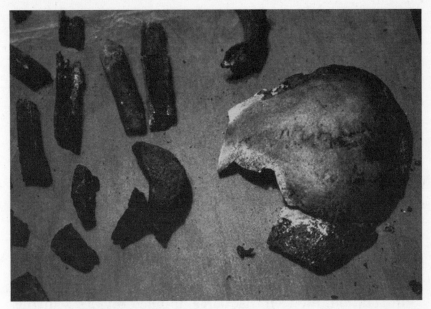

Bone fragments recovered from the burning car were almost ash, but loaded with information.

To get answers investigators turned to Dr. William Bass, one of the most respected forensic anthropologists in the world. He was given the charred bits of the body recovered from the vehicle. Of particular interest were a skull fragment about the size of a playing card and four teeth.

A simple visual examination of the skull fragment revealed something unusual: the fragment was burned on the inside, but there were no burn marks on the outside. How was this possible? If the driver had been consumed by fire it seemed obvious that the outside of his skull would be more exposed to flames than the inside. Dr. Bass said there was a simple explanation. He told investigators that the head of the victim was in the least burnt portion of the car—the floor. The victim, he said, was upside down, which led to another conclusion: the scene had been staged.

The skull fragment also provided clues about the victim's

age. The human skull has twenty-eight different plate-like bones. These bones come together in a process called "fusion" that looks much like the stitching on clothes. As a person grows older that stitching, or "fusion," tends to disappear. In the skull fragment recovered from the crash the fusion was almost non-existent, which told Dr. Bass that the victim is not in his mid-thirties like Madison Rutherford, but somewhere closer to his mid-fifties.

It got stranger. Different races have different characteristics in their dentition, or teeth. Two of the teeth recovered from the vehicle were incisors, and they had a distinctive shovel shape on the back side. This was not something normally associated with a Caucasian, like Madison Rutherford. It was more common to someone of Asian descent or a Native American.

In addition, the teeth had large, unfilled cavities, which is not something normally associated with a wealthy financial analyst with plenty of disposable income. And in fragments from the joints and spine that were also recovered, Dr. Bass saw a great deal of wear. This said to him that the bones belonged to someone who had engaged in years of manual labor.

He told the insurance companies his results. The bones from the burned-out car did not belong to a wealthy, relatively young, white man. They most likely belonged to a fifty-to sixty-year-old Mexican peasant from, in his words, "the lower socio-economic level."

This raised more questions than it answered. Who did the bones belong to? And where was Madison Rutherford?

Mexican officials were told of Dr. Bass's findings, and they began their own investigation. They soon determined that the body in the vehicle had been stolen. Rural Mexico has a great many above-ground tombs, and it appeared that someone had simply slipped the cement top of one of the crypts and pulled out a skeleton, which was then deposited in the vehicle. Grave robbing was not uncommon, so it was impossible to identify

He assured Brigitte that the FBI sting would soon be over, that he would come out of hiding, and everything would be okay. But he warned her in no uncertain terms that she was to say nothing about seeing him alive. He said the Mafia might be watching and if that if she blew his cover, rumors of his death would soon become more than just rumors. He then disappeared into the woods behind her house.

Brigitte believed him, and kept quiet. The insurance companies, on the other hand, were not privy to Madison's story, and wouldn't have believed it if they were. They brought in the FBI, which had begun following Rhynie Rutherford to see if she might lead them to Madison. This turned up nothing, but a search of her car records yielded a potential clue. One of her cars was being driven by a financial planner . . . in Boston. His name was Thomas Bey Hamilton.

Investigators thought this might be their man and put him under surveillance. Photographs of Madison and Mr. Hamilton seemed to indicate they were the same person. The name, they found, was one of a series of aliases—all with a link to major figures in American history. It turned out that Madison Rutherford was born John Sankey, but apparently liked presidential-sounding names—Madison, Rutherford, Hamilton. A little over a year after being found "dead," Mr. Sankey-Madison-Rutherford-Hamilton was arrested on a charge of fraud.

This was devastating news for Brigitte Beck. Madison was a con man, not an undercover agent for the FBI. And she was one of the people he conned. Her entire life savings had been used by Madison to play the stock market during the boom of the late 1990s. When the boom went bust, Brigitte lost all her money. Since she'd signed over power of attorney, there was nothing she or the law could do about it.

Police monitored Madison's phone calls from prison, and his first call was to his wife. He gave her instructions that made it clear she had been part of the fraud all along. She was arrested a short time later and refused to cooperate with police—until she found out she was the victim of a different type of fraud. Police played for her tape recorded conversations of Madison with various girlfriends. In some he said he was unmarried; in others he described Rhynie as "fat" and "old" and said a divorce was imminent.

That was enough for Rhynie Rutherford. She changed her mind and told the FBI everything they wanted to know. For Madison the game was up. Knowing he would be convicted he decided to plead guilty. Federal sentencing guidelines limited his sentence to five years. Rhynie served eighteen months. Brigitte Beck was left with less than $500 and no hope for the cozy retirement she had planned. When we left her, she was considering selling her house to support herself or moving back to Germany so her family could help support her.

The old saying "there's a fine line between bravery and stupidity" is perhaps the best epitaph for this case. Madison's story was certainly audacious, but it all hinged on the insurance companies' willingness to shell out millions of dollars on the strength of a quickie accident report from Mexican authorities. It's unlikely they would ever do so, and subsequent events proved they would go to some lengths before parting with their money. But it was a brave plan—especially if you discount the stupid parts.

Perhaps the most stupid part surfaced when FBI agents searched the Boston apartment of Madison's last alias, Thomas Bey Hamilton. In his belongings they found a number of books on how to change identities, some travel information on Mexico, and in one of his notebooks they found a "to do" list for the calendar year 2000. At the top of the list, under "Goals for 2000," Madison wrote the following: "Collect seven million dollars from insurance company."

The FBI agent we interviewed for this story laughed so hard when he told us this that we had to temporarily stop the inter-

Madison Rutherford's mug shot. The man of many identities takes on a new one: felon.

with any certainty who the bones belonged to.

Meanwhile, the insurance companies were now convinced that Madison Rutherford was alive, and they started asking questions of friends, family members, and clients, like Brigitte Beck. For her, news that Madison might be scamming the insurance companies was alarming—it could spell her financial ruin. She tried to get answers, but Madison's wife Rhynie said she didn't know where he was.

Soon, however, Brigitte Beck's questions about Madison's whereabouts were put to rest. One night he turned up at her doorstep and slipped inside her house. He told her an incredible story. He said that he was working undercover with the FBI in a sting operation aimed at a large scale Mafia drug-running outfit. He was helping the Mafia launder its drug money, and when the Mafia began to suspect he was working for the FBI his "handlers" came up with a way to make it look like he had been killed.

view. Before this he had been the picture of a calm, cool law enforcement professional, but this bit of inside information proved too much. If you see this episode you can see him struggle to keep from laughing.

Madison and Rhynie's story got even stranger. They were both influenced by astrology, so much so that friends said it was not uncommon for them to change plans depending on the alignment of the stars. Shortly after Madison was arrested he made his phone call to Rhynie. As he faces an almost certain prison term, the first thing he does is ask her if "the moon is still in Sagittarius." She's got other things on her mind, and proceeds to tell him that she's terrified. It's only then that he gives her instructions on how to cover up their scam.

As for Brigitte Beck, the tragedy of her story is all too apparent on camera. Her grief at the loss of her financial security is heartbreaking to see. She brought friends over to provide emotional support as she told her story, but telling the whole thing from beginning to end—something she had never really done before—proved almost too much for her. Later we had to get what's known as an "introduction shot" of her. We'd show some video of her walking around her house that would introduce her into the show. It was a rainy day, and she asked the producer what she should be thinking about while we shot the video. He told her to think about what happened to her, and when she did she broke down in tears, all of which is in the episode.

Brigitte's friends continue to rally around her and are lobbying local representatives to see if they can do something to help her keep her house, but when we last talked, her financial future was far from certain.

One other strange thing about this episode concerns the re-creations. This story happened in Mexico during the summer. Unhappily for us, we shot the re-creations in late December in eastern Pennsylvania during a bitter cold snap. The actor who played Madison Rutherford had to act as if he were staging his own death during a hot Mexican night. He's in a T-shirt on a Pennsylvania night with sub-zero wind-chill. It was brutal, especially when you realize that before each take he had to suck on a mouthful of ice cubes to cool his breath. That was the only way to keep his breath from vaporizing in the winter cold, which would be a dead giveaway that we were shooting in winter. We tried to cover the area where we shot the scene in fake fog, but if you take a close look you might realize we were a long, long way from Mexico in the summertime.

While Madison Rutherford was cold, calculating, and ruthless, some of these "pretenders"—despite appearing normal to friends and coworkers—simply can't control their compulsions. Take the case of Paul Keller, which we called "Fire Proof."

On August 9, 1992, the resources of the Seattle Fire Department were stretched to the limit. Three churches, located within a few miles of each other, were engulfed in flames. After the fires had been extinguished, arson dogs were brought to the smoldering scenes to search for flammable liquids, but none were found. Experts discovered no evidence of accelerants, and there was no sign of vandalism. All of the fires started the same way: on the ground floor, at chest level. During the next several weeks, eight churches—six of them Lutheran—were set on fire.

Soon businesses and homes also became targets. In one night alone, there were twelve different arson fires. Many of the homeowners lost all of their possessions, barely escaping with their lives.

By the fall, the arsonist had set more than twenty-five fires. Residents formed neighborhood groups to protect their houses, and fire companies patrolled throughout the night, but still the fires continued. A task force was formed, and a psychological profile of the arsonist was commissioned. The profiler predicted the arsonist would be a white male, in his late teens or early twenties, who abused alcohol or drugs. He would be intelligent but also an underachiever who had recently experienced a major trauma in his life. He would be working as a salesperson or delivery person, which would account for his familiarity with the area.

The arsonist left behind no clues until fire number twenty-eight, when two fingerprints were discovered near the window where the fire began. The prints were compared with hundreds of thousands on file. No match was found, so the arsonist probably did not have a criminal record. Two weeks later, at fire number forty-two, investigators found urine nearby, in the snow. It was carefully collected for DNA testing, but the melting snow made it impossible to extract a sample for analysis.

The fires continued. Then, just after midnight on September 22, 1992, the arsonist took on his biggest target to date. He hit a home for senior citizens that housed more than four hundred residents. Three elderly women, all of them over eighty years old, died in the blaze. The arsonist was now also a killer, and the community was terrorized.

The press coverage was extensive, and the task force got thousands of potential leads. One in particular stood out because the suspect fit the physical description provided by the psychological profile. A woman told investigators that a man bumped into her near one of the fires. The man appeared to be drunk and was well dressed. She glimpsed his license plate, but didn't write down the numbers. The incident had occurred weeks earlier, and her recollection of the man's appearance had faded.

The woman seemed credible, and with fires starting almost every night, investigators decided to try something that had only been used a few times before, and had never been used in such a high-profile case. They decided the woman be an excellent candidate for forensic hypnosis. The simple definition of hypnosis is that is focuses the mind on one area. Las Vegas entertainers who hypnotize members of the audience will focus on their imaginations; forensic scientists focus on memory.

The forensic hypnotist will search for "triggers" to unlock the memory of the witness. Most often these triggers will be sensory—the feel of a fabric, a distinctive sound, an unusual smell. Anyone who has smelled something and had the scent transport them back to another place and time will know exactly what a forensic hypnotist means by a memory trigger.

In the case of the fire investigation, the hypnotist focused the unconscious mind of the witness on the alcohol she said she smelled on the well-dressed man. Once hypnotized she was lead through the events of that night. She recalled the man was wearing an Oxford shirt and had bumped into her near an ATM machine. He mentioned the rash of fires. He walked to a large car, which she thought might be blue but wasn't sure.

When asked if she could remember the license plate number she provided the first thing that came to her mind: She said the plate began with the letter "K," and contained an "M" and the number "4." This was good information, but since four million cars in northern Washington had plates with that combination investigators needed something more. So they brought in a composite artist named John Hinds.

With the woman still under hypnosis Hinds had her divide the man's face into sections. Bit by bit, section by section, Hinds pulled details from the witness. The eyes were "narrow." The hair was "pushed back off his head." He wore "thin, wire glasses." After about two hours Hinds showed the drawing to the witness. She made some minor changes. When it was finished she was confident it looked like the man she saw at the scene of the fire.

The question now was: what next? If the drawing were released to the public the arsonist might recognize himself and go into hiding. The case would never be solved and people would continue to live in fear that their house could be torched at any time. There was also a distinct possibility that the arsonist would be so enraged by seeing his picture that he'd step up his activity and possibly claim more lives. Eventually investigators decided they had to go public with the photo. Hundreds of thousands of people would see it and just one might finally recognize the firebug terrorizing the community.

On January 27, 1993, the task force held a news conference in which three composite drawings—the one from their witness and two "dummy" drawings to draw off hoax callers—were broadcast on local television. A day later they got a call from a tearful father, a pillar of the local business community who feared he knew the arsonist. He thought it might be his son.

George Keller, owner of a local advertising agency, told police that his son Paul bore a striking resemblance to the person in the drawing. George examined cell phone records and credit card receipts and discovered his son had been nearby when the fires were set. Paul Keller was twenty-seven years old and employed in the family advertising business. He was the oldest of three children in a devoutly Lutheran family. Paul Keller's sales routes were in the areas where the fires had occurred. Almost everyone who knew him described Keller as a kind, respectful, God-fearing member of the community.

But as his father continued his story, investigators were stunned. Paul Keller fit the psychological profile to a "t." His father said that from an early age Paul was obsessed with fire, and had actually started a fairly large one when he was only nine years old. He had applied for a job as a fire fighter but had been rejected. He was intelligent but had not done well in school. He abused alcohol. And most important the one unusual prediction in the profile—that the firebug would have recently suffered emotional trauma—was true in Paul Keller's case. His wife was divorcing him, and he had recently filed for

118

bankruptcy.

The kicker was that he drove a large blue car, the license plate began with the letter "K," and contained the number "4" and the letter "M." The details obtained by forensic hypnosis were uncannily accurate.

Police hoped to catch Paul Keller in the act, and he was placed under surveillance. But after ten days, he was taken into custody. Initially, he said he was innocent, but when investigators complimented him by saying he was the best arsonist they'd every seen, he confessed to setting seventy-five fires—including the fire at the retirement home. His fingerprints matched those found at one of the crime scenes. His technique was surprisingly simple. He would walk up to the site and use a cigarette lighter to torch up fiberglass awnings or pieces of trash that he knew would burn easily.

Shortly after his confession, Paul Keller was convicted of arson and murder. He will not be eligible for parole until he is 113 years old.

The Bureau of Alcohol, Tobacco, Firearms and Explosives (ATF), in tandem with local police departments across the greater Seattle area, bore the brunt of this investigation. And it was brutalizing. Six months of dealing with the fears of a community on edge, and of coping with the fact that no significant clues were found at any of the fire scenes took its toll on investigators. In the months after Paul Keller's arrest, there were marriage breakups, some nervous breakdowns, and a lot of early retirements.

Almost a decade had passed by the time we caught up with members of the task force, and they were still reluctant to talk about the case. One of them was an intimidating character built like an inside linebacker. With a crew cut and rigid posture, his bearing was distinctly military. But he was reduced to tears as he talked about the unseen effects of Paul Keller's arson spree. "You can't believe how many lives that guy screwed up," he told us. He spoke about an elderly woman who had taken great pride in her independence. After her house burned down she was forced to move back in with her children. She died shortly afterward. She was unhurt in the fire, but her family said it just broke her spirit. She'd survived a lot of things, but having to start from scratch while in her mid-eighties was just too much for her to bear.

As for Paul Keller, he is, as the psychological profiler said, an articulate, intelligent man. Watch the episode and see for yourself. It's chilling. The ATF, wanting to make sure that absolutely nothing in this investigation was left to chance, videotaped every interview with him. And in a stroke of good fortune, they made those tapes available to *Forensic Files*. As ATF agents take Keller to various fire scenes you can see the almost child-like glee as he describes how each one was set. You can see how eager he is for approval, and you can see what happens when Keller's interrogators follow the detailed instructions of the psychological profilers.

They told investigators to make Keller feel like a "VIP or some head of state." So after he was arrested Keller was brought into custody in the middle of a train of police and fire department vehicles, all with their sirens on and their lights flashing. He arrived to find as many officers as could be made available. Keller literally walked a gauntlet—it this case it was more like a receiving line—of local law enforcement officials before getting to the interrogation room. The intention was to build him up as much as possible so that he couldn't resist taking credit for his crimes.

Once inside, with tapes rolling, you can see investigators trying to soften him up. After a few minutes, this exchange took place.

Keller: "You guys don't think I'm a bad guy, do you?"

ATF agent: "You are absolutely fascinating to us. We respect you for what you've been able to do here. It's amazing."

Paul Keller and the composite drawing that identified him. A striking resemblance.

You can see Keller's body language change. This is what he's been waiting for. A minute later, he confesses and then adds: "I know you guys are thrilled that I'm sitting here. And I'm thrilled to be sitting here."

Another interesting aspect of this particular episode is the forensic hypnosis. Usually we attempt to re-create what really happened in a given story. This time we were attempting to re-create what was essentially a hypnotically-induced dream. As the witness dredges up the license plate numbers from her subconscious we were able to employ a lot of nice visual effects to show how the plate began to take shape in her mind. It's one of only two times in the history of the program where we've re-created a "dream."

As for the composite drawing, when you see it side by side with Paul Keller's photograph you'll likely become a believer in how effective it is as an investigative tool. The resemblance is uncanny, especially when you consider that the source was a hypnotic dream. One can only imagine what it was like for Paul Keller's father—already worried that his son might be the firebug—to turn on the TV and see the drawing that confirmed all his worst fears. The man ended up losing his business, making sure his son was adequately defended in court.

The police composite artist, John Hinds, had retired when we caught up with him. We assumed he was an artist before he got into composite drawing. "No, no, no," he insisted. "I couldn't draw anything." Intrigued by how well it worked in a case early in his career he prevailed upon his superiors to let him take a month-long training course to see if he had any aptitude. Many years, and many composite drawings later, he whiles away his retirement, creating detailed portraits of friends, family, and a number of paying customers. When asked if he thought his drawing of Paul Keller was "art," Hinds only laughed and said, "Yeah, in a way."

While Paul Keller fit the psychological profile in his case, there are some Great Pretenders who defy that sort of analysis. Take a case we called "Unholy Vows," a rare instance in which *Forensic Files* went back in history.

When Valerian Trifa applied for citizenship in the U.S. after World War II, he told immigration officials a gruesome story of time he had spent in a concentration camp during the war. He claimed the Nazis imprisoned him in the Dachau concentration camp because of deeply held religious beliefs and his outspoken opposition to the war. He was soon granted residency status and soon afterward settled near Detroit, where he became a Romanian Orthodox priest. He rose quickly through the hierarchy of a church whose membership had swelled with the influx of Trifa's fellow refugees.

Father Trifa was a staunch anti-communist, and vocal supporter of the U. S. Cold War policy. He was so outspoken that Richard Nixon, then vice-president invited him to say the commencement prayer in the U.S. Senate chambers in 1955. Two years later Trifa was named Archbishop of the Romanian Orthodox Church of America, a powerful post that put him at the head of more than 35,000 parishioners nationwide. It was a remarkable rise for a man who had entered the country a penniless refugee.

But his rise was not without its problems. The same year he was named Archbishop, an alleged incident from Trifa's past came back to haunt him. He was linked to one of the most notorious attacks of anti-Semitism in the entire war. Witnesses said that while a young man in Romania, Trifa was student leader of an organization known as the Legion of the Order of the Archangel Michael, an ultra-nationalist, militaristic, and virulently anti-Semitic group based in his home city of Bucharest. These witnesses told U.S. authorities that on January 20, 1941, Trifa gave a radio address calling for the replacement of all "Judah-like Masons" in the Romanian government. His speech touched off four days of rioting that culminated in some three hundred Jews being killed in a kosher slaughterhouse. These murders were particularly gruesome: all the victims had their throats cut in a parody of the traditional Jewish method of slaughtering animals.

Witnesses claimed that the man who was now Romanian Archbishop of Detroit was in fact the same man who had set off the slaughter. They told U.S. Immigration officials that Trifa had been tried in absentia in Romania and sentenced to life in prison with hard labor for crimes against humanity.

The question facing the U.S. government was simple—was the highly placed religious figure now living outside Detroit the same hate monger who had caused the deaths of hundreds of Jews? Had he lied about his background in entering the U.S.? And if so, how could it be proven?

Witness upon witness swore he was the same man, but in the search from some concrete proof investigators turned to handwriting analysis, the only tool at their disposal. They had current documents from Archbishop Trifa and documents that were confirmed to have been written by the alleged anti-Semite from Bucharest. Analyst Gideon Epstein compared the documents and told investigators that he was convinced the anti-Semitic murderer and the Romanian Archbishop were the same man.

This, however, was not definitive proof. It was certainly not enough to have Trifa—still a highly placed, and even revered religious figure—deported.

Still, it was enough to convince U.S. Immigration officials that the witness accounts were accurate—that Archbishop Trifa had incited a murderous anti-Semitic rampage, and had lied about it when he entered the country. For his part, Archbishop Trifa made his position explicitly clear: the accounts of his fellow refugees could not be proven, and he would fight all extradition efforts in court. Most analysts agreed that since the U.S. government had nothing definitive against the Archbishop he was likely to win.

U.S. government officials asked their counterparts in what was then West Germany if they had any documentation on Trifa. In May 1982, after searching its archives, the West Germans found documents they thought might be linked to Trifa, and they were turned over to the FBI's Identification Division. Most of them were postcards, all written from a health spa in Nazi Germany. They had Trifa's signature and the handwriting was deemed to be his. This certainly belied his claim that he was being held at Dachau.

But again, U.S. officials faced the same problem: there was no conclusive way to prove the cards had been written by Trifa.

But forensic analysts became interested in one particular postcard. It was dated January 14, 1942, and was almost blank. The writer, apparently Trifa, wanted his friends back in Romania to have the address of the health spa so that they could

Valerian Trifa early in his priesthood. A religious figure with a hate-filled past.

write to him if they chose, and only supplied the address and his signature. The card appeared to have the faint imprint of a thumb, but analysts couldn't be sure.

The FBI wanted to analyze the postcard further, but the West German government had issued strict instructions that the documents they provided not be damaged or altered in any way. At that time the only way to reveal a latent print was to "dust" the document, which meant that trying to lift a print from the card would inevitably cause some damage. The West Germans denied permission.

The FBI was in a quandary until they turned to a newly developed forensic tool: laser technology. The fact that lasers would make certain prints visible was accidentally discovered in Canada in the mid-1970s. It seemed that every time Canadian researchers employed lasers they ran into problems because the lasers reacted with the residue left by human finger oils. The fingerprints of researchers would glow and provide visibility problems. The technology was quickly incorporated by law enforcement agencies around the world to lift fingerprints because it is quick, accurate, and non-invasive.

Lasers were found to be particularly effective with older evidence.While the visual aspects of a print would often degrade, the oils would not. The laser technology would not harm the postcard in any way, so the West Germans were now perfectly willing to turn it over for further examination.

In 1982, forty years after the postcard had been sent, it was placed under the FBI's newly acquired laser. On the large, blank area in the center of the postcard, analysts found a small, perfectly formed thumbprint glowing under the laser light. The print was photographed, and analysts went back to the document Valerian Trifa had filled out before being allowed into the U.S. in 1950—a document which included fingerprints made by the Immigration Service.

The thumbprint on the postcard and the immigration document were identical. This was conclusive—the postcard, sent from Nazi Germany in 1942, had definitely been handled by Valerian Trifa. What this meant for immigration officials was that Trifa had clearly lied when he entered the country. He was not a prisoner in Dachau; he was a guest at a Nazi-run health spa. The U.S. government moved to deport him.

Archbishop Trifa desperately searched for a country that would take him in, all the time maintaining his innocence. He was finally deported to Portugal, where he died in 1987. In the end, the highly respected religious figure could not escape his own history. The past he tried so hard to keep hidden had finally been exposed by the latest in forensic technology.

The thumbprint—a copy of the actual photograph can be seen in our program—is the oldest latent print ever lifted. This was quite a coup for the FBI. Immigration had been trying for the better part of twenty years to get Trifa kicked out of the country. Many of his fellow Romanian exiles and particularly the Romanian Jewish community was outraged not only that he was living lavishly in the U.S., but that he had pawned himself off as religious leader.

As you can imagine, the Romanian Orthodox church was not happy about us doing this story. Trifa still had many supporters in the church. They claimed he was a changed man and had renounced his past. The producer on this episode made a number of calls to church officials to see if they would be willing to cooperate. They flatly refused, and one exchange best sums up their feelings about the story.

A church official, a man who had met and worked with Archbishop Trifa a number of times, became exasperated with our producer, finally asking if he "believed in the risen Christ."

The producer, a Catholic high school graduate, answered that as a matter of fact he did. Then why, the priest wanted to know, could the producer not accept the fact Trifa had turned his life around by becoming a servant of the Church? The producer replied that he was perfectly happy to accept Trifa's conversion, but that his past was still relevant. The producer then read from an anti-Semitic pamphlet written by Trifa in the early 1940s. The pamphlet contained the entire panoply of racial epithets directed against Jews. It was an extraordinarily ugly, hate-filled document.

The phone went quiet, and the priest asked, "are you sure Archbishop Trifa wrote that?" The producer replied he was positive, that there was documentation from U.S., Romanian, and even Nazi archives that identified Trifa as the author. The priest sighed, said simply that he could understand why the case remained of interest, wished the producer good luck with the story, and asked him never to call again.

Someone for whom the past remains very much alive is Eli Rosenbaum, the prosecutor who helped get Trifa deported. Rosenbaum works for the U.S. government's Office of Special

Investigations (OSI), an arm of the Justice Department specifically charged with hunting down war criminals. In a nondescript office building he and a small, tightly knit group of prosecutors and investigators scour the world for former Nazis and Nazi sympathizers who've escaped justice.

And if his desk is any indication, there's plenty of work to do. The producer on this story told us that about thirty pounds of documents sat on Rosenbaum's desk—all from open cases. When our crew tried to move some of these documents for a shot Rosenbaum was adamant. "Don't move anything," he said. "It looks like a mess but, believe me, I know where everything is." The shot of him behind his desk is in our program, and is a video testament to the size of Rosenbaum's workload and his unusual powers of organization.

One more interesting thing about this story is that it features one of the best pieces of "prop" evidence we've ever used. The postcard that contained the thumbprint was returned to the German archives and was not available for us to use. So we needed something that would allow viewers to see how a thumbprint on a postcard could be visualized with laser technology. We called the FBI which, as always, was cooperative. Our producers offered to mock up something, but the FBI said they would take care of it. We weren't sure they would give us something that would work—they are, after all, in the business of catching bad guys and we're in the TV business—but they assured us that the perfect prop would be ready for us.

On the day we arrived for taping the producer asked to see what they had, thinking that if it was unacceptable there was still time to find something that would do the job. The FBI laser technician produced a photocopied version of the actual postcard that he had glued over a piece of cardboard. The result was a prop that looked exactly like the forty-year-old postcard that had been taken from the West German archives. Our producer was impressed and thanked the technician pro-

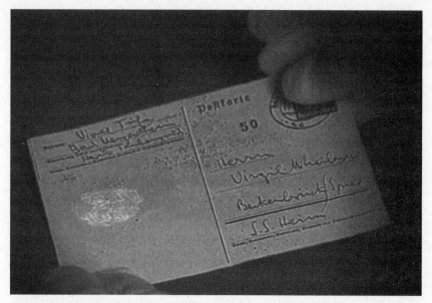

The forty-year-old thumbprint that revealed Father Trifa's true identity as a Nazi sympathizer.

fusely. The technician smiled. "Wait," he said, "it only gets better." The man was obviously proud of his work and we soon saw why.

The "prop" postcard was placed under the laser. Once a filter that eliminates all light other than the laser was put in place a beautiful, crystal clear thumbprint emerged on the postcard. We were stunned and knew right away that this would look spectacular on camera. For his part, the technician was as happy as we were. "It's the same size," he told us, " and in the same exact position as the original Trifa print." If you ever see this episode, make sure to check it out. Talk about history coming to life.

Archbishop Trifa is among the definitive "Great Pretenders," but sadly, he's got some serious competition.

A case we called "Honor thy Father" shows why.

In the early 1980s, sixty-year-old Zein Isa and his wife Maria emigrated from Palestine with their family. They supported themselves with a small grocery store in downtown St. Louis, and Zein gave every appearance of being a good neighbor and honest businessman. Zein was passionate about the Palestinian cause, so much so that he named his youngest daughter, "Palestina." Known to friends as Tina, she was a popular, straight "A" high school junior who dreamed of attending college and becoming an airline pilot.

Her father had other plans. For him, her future was as a stay-at-home mother, and he felt there would be no need for her to go to college. Her embrace of the American lifestyle enraged him. He hated her clothes, he hated her independence, and he particularly hated her earning spending money through a job at a fast-food restaurant. Things between father and daughter came to a head when he found out she had a boyfriend, something he feared would compromise her ability to get a traditional Palestinian husband.

On November 6, 1989, Tina returned from working the night shift at her job. According to her parents, they confronted her about working and she became belligerent. She told them she wanted to live on her own, and she demanded that her parents give her $5,000. When they refused, Tina pulled a knife from her backpack and threatened them. During the struggle which followed, Zein said, his daughter came at him with the knife and tried to kill him. He said he wrestled the knife away from her and then killed her in self-defense. Zein Isa was covered with blood, and had what appeared to be defensive wounds on his hands.

The medical examiner used a process called "wound pattern analysis" to try and figure out what happened. Tina had sustained six deep stab wounds to her lower central chest and abdomen—all the wounds close together. What this said to the examiner was that while Tina was being attacked she either stayed completely still of her own volition or—and this was the more likely theory—that she had been restrained. The examiner's theory was supported by the paramedics who were first on the scene. They said that when they found Tina's body her arms were above her head, as if she someone had held them . It was unlikely that Zein could have held Tina down and attacked her at the same time. The only other person in the room was Tina's mother, Maria. She said she sat horrified on the sofa during the entire attack, but had no explanation for the fact that Tina's blood and hair were found on the inside of the sweater she was wearing.

It got worse. Investigators turned to the wounds on Zein's hands, which he said were defensive. They were clean and deep cuts to the bottom of his palm. Defensive wounds are usually shallow slashes, inflicted when the victim throws up his or her hands to deflect a blow. The wounds to Zein's hands gave every appearance that he had been holding the knife. Given the other evidence, investigators theorized that his hands had become so bloody during the attack that they had been cut as they slipped down the blade.

But who could kill one's own daughter in such a brutal fashion? Investigators decided to bone up on their cultural history, and they found that such events are not without precedent in Middle Eastern culture. Scholars familiar with the case told investigators that Tina Isa's death may have been what's known as an "honor killing." While getting a job and dating are common in the United States, such activities in parts of the Middle East where arranged marriages are the norm, it is considered unacceptable behavior. If Tina's parents felt she had stained the family's honor, centuries of tradition dictated a brutal response: "Blood must cleanse blood." Only Tina's death could restore the family's honor.

This seemed to provide a motive. In addition, the evidence clearly indicated that Zein Isa had killed his daughter, and that his wife had helped him. But prosecutors faced a host of problems. The crime was so horrific they didn't know if a jury would believe that otherwise loving parents could murder their own child simply because she had a job and a boyfriend. They feared the cultural difference between jury and suspects might be insurmountable.

While they mulled their options they got an unexpected call from the FBI. It turned out that counter-terrorism officials were familiar with Zein Isa. He was suspected of having ties to terrorist cells and was know to have attended a meeting in Mexico with known terrorists, all of whom where connected to the Palestine Liberation Organization and to the international terror broker, Abu Nidal. During a two-year period, Zein had made fourteen trips to different foreign cities.

Under provisions of the Foreign Intelligence Surveillance Act, Zein's home had been wiretapped. For twenty-four hours a day, seven days a week his activities and those of his family had been tape-recorded by the FBI. The FBI been sporadically monitoring the recordings, and didn't know what was on all of them. But Tina's murder happened inside the house and they knew the date and time. A quick perusal of the tapes revealed the murder had been recorded.

But there was yet another problem. The FBI was reluctant to release the tapes, fearing their electronic surveillance of other suspected terrorists would be compromised. St. Louis prosecutors pleaded their case: the evidence indicated that an innocent girl had been murdered in cold blood, and without the tapes it appeared likely the killers—the girl's parents—would walk away. Attorney General Richard Thornberg finally relented and the tapes were turned over to the St. Louis police.

What they revealed was chilling. Several weeks before Tina was killed, Zein conspired with a relative about how to make Tina's death appear to be an accident. The tapes also revealed that how wide the gulf between Americanized Tina and her

Evidence photo of Zein Isa minutes after he killed his own daughter. The wounds on his hands showed it wasn't self defense.

traditional parents had become. Tina's mother and father talked incessantly about her job, her boyfriend, and what they could do to restore the family's honor. The tapes made it clear that things were building to a head.

When Tina came home on the night of her death, her parents had planned to confront her and if she didn't agree to change her ways, to kill her. Tina, not realizing the gravity of the situation, argued with her parents like a typical teenager. Voices were raised and soon Zein told his daughter she was going to die. He then went into the kitchen and grabbed a knife. Tina screamed, and pleaded with her mother for help. Her mother told her to shut up, and then held her down while her father stabbed her to death. After the initial stabbings, Zein went to the kitchen to get another knife to finish the job. Contrary to his account, Tina did not demand $5,000, nor did the tape contain any reference to Tina having a knife.

Zein and Maria Isa were found guilty of first-degree murder and each was sentenced to death. In 1998, before the sentence could be carried out, Zein died in prison from natural causes. Maria's death sentence was later reversed on a technicality, but she will spend the rest of her life in prison with no possibility of parole.

If you've never seen this episode, be forewarned: the audio tape is likely to make your blood run cold. It's vital to the story, and we felt that as a result we had an obligation to play at least parts of it. It's in Arabic with English-language subtitles, but even without the subtitles it's rough going. Even seasoned homicide detectives said it was one of the most disturbing things they'd ever heard.

Here's a portion of the transcript that starts just after Tina enters the home. She closes the door and gets this greeting from her mother:

Maria: "Where were you, bitch?

The family begins to argue. Tina's parents confront her about her decision to work outside the home. Tina refuses to back down, and says she won't quit her job. Her father is enraged:

Zein: "You are a She-devil! So you've made up your mind? You're going to stay this way? You've decided that you're going to keep living this way?"

Tina responds by daring her parents to throw her out of the

house, and the argument escalates. Finally, her father has had enough. He does what he has planned all along, and threatens Tina.

Zein: "Here, listen my dear daughter. Do you know that this is the last day? That tonight you're going to die?"

Tina: "What?"

Seconds later Tina starts screaming and then pleads with her mother for help.

Tina: "Mother! Please help me!"

Maria: "What? What do you mean?

Zein: "Keep still, Tina!"

Tina: (screaming) "Help! Help!"

As Tina is held by her mother her father stabs her. As she lay dying she gets one last order from her controlling father.

Zein: "Quiet, little one. Die, my daughter, die."

At no place on the tape does Tina initiate an attack on her parents. In fact, the tapes reveal something even more startling. As she pleads with her mother for help, she gets this response:

Maria. "What? Help? Shut up."

Incredibly, the murder takes about ten minutes. Tina's parents wait a half-hour before calling an ambulance.

The whole thing is so horrific that the re-creation in our episode is shot through a curtain. There's a gauzy quality that hides all of the violence. After all, the audio tape makes what happened all too clear.

Zein's neighbors, of course, said they couldn't believe he was capable of such an act. And by all accounts he went to his grave believing Tina had brought her murder upon herself and that his actions were completely justified.

The same couldn't be said for another "pillar of the community," an international con man we featured on a story called "Time Will Tell." It could just as well be called "The Name Game," since the perpetrator changed names the way some people change cars.

On July 28, 1996, two fishermen pulling in their nets off the southwest coast of England made a gruesome discovery. Entangled in their nets was a ten-pound anchor and a man's decomposing body. The fishermen contacted the authorities about the body, but one of the men, thinking the anchor was of little value to investigators, pawned it for a few pounds' cash.

A police surgeon sent to inspect the body found a gash on the back of the head and bruising on the left hip. Owing to the state of decomposition, the surgeon concluded that the body could not have been at sea for more than a week. A subsequent autopsy cited drowning as the cause of death, but no determination could be made as to whether the death was a murder or an accident and whether the wounds to the body were caused pre- or post-mortem. Police ran the victim's fingerprints and found no matches; this also held true with his dental impressions.

There were two main clues to the victim's identity. The first was a watch—a Rolex Oyster Perpetual Chronometer. This watch had to be wound by hand every day, and had stopped on July 21, which led to speculation that the victim probably died on July 20. The second was a maple leaf tattoo—a Canadian flag—on the top of his right hand.

The victim was dubbed "The Rolex Man" by the press and there was considerable pressure to come up with an identity. Investigators turned to the watch. All Rolexes are imprinted with a serial number, and when this particular watch was traced it was found to have belonged to one Ronald Platt.

Police went to Platt's last known address. Neighbors told them that Platt had recently moved to France and that they could probably get more information from his closest friend, a man named David Davis who lived nearby.

Police went to question Davis, but called at the wrong house. The man who greeted them at that house said there was no David Davis in his neighborhood. This man said the owner of the house police meant to visit was named Ronald Platt. But the man answering the door identified himself as David Davis and told them that Platt had left for France.

Investigators were confused—and suspicious. So they did a background search centering on the deeds to the home and other legal documents. They noticed that the signature "Ronald Platt" was markedly different on many of the documents. This led to speculation that someone was masquerading as Mr. Platt, and that this person might be David Davis—especially since people in the neighborhood told them that Davis was known to them as Ronald Platt. They said "Davis/Platte" lived with his young wife, Noelle, who was said to be melancholy and subservient to her husband.

Police did simultaneous checks on "Platt" and "Davis." The first clue came with Ronald Platt's ex-girlfriend, a woman named Elaine Boyes. She told investigators that years earlier she and Ronald Platt had worked for David Davis. Her main job was to transfer large sums of money to various Swiss bank accounts for his company, the Cavendish Corporation. She said that she and Platt had wanted to move back to their native Canada in 1993, and that this move was financed by David Davis.

But prospects in Canada were bleak and both Boyes and "Platt" moved back to England just weeks before fisherman dredged up the body that had sparked the investigation. Police speculated that David Davis had sent Platt back to Canada so that he could assume Platt's identity in England. With the money in the Swiss bank accounts, Davis would be comfortable, wealthy, and able to start all over. But when Platt returned to England this plan was foiled—a possible motive for murder.

Police went to arrest "David Davis" on suspicion of murder. Upon arriving at his house they found his wife, Noelle, attempting to hide a large quantity of gold bullion. Both Davis and Noelle were taken into custody and their house and boat were searched. In the home police found $50,000 worth of gold bars and large amounts of currency. They also found a false ID in the name of Ronald Platt and a birth certificate for Noelle's nine-month old daughter, Lily. The father was listed as Ronald Platt, and the mother as Elaine Boyes. In the boat police found three human head hairs lying on a pillow; some skin was found at the end of one hair and was sent for DNA analysis. The boat was also equipped with a GPS Navigational Aerial—a device that stores data on the boat's previous trips.

With "David Davis" in custody, police were able to run his prints through Interpol. What they found was that "Davis" was in fact named Albert Walker, and that Walker was Number Four on Interpol's Most Wanted List. Walker was facing charges of embezzling more than three million dollars from his firm, Walker Investment Corporation of Canada. When he fled he was believed to have taken his daughter, Sheena, with him. When confronted, "Noelle" said she was Sheena.

The DNA taken from the hair found in Albert Walker's boat matched the DNA from the body found by the fisherman. The background search on Ronald Platt yielded photos, but the body was too decomposed for a visual match. However, the tattoo on his wrist, in combination with the serial number on the Rolex, was enough to positively identify the body as Ronald Platt. An analysis of the boat's navigational system showed that it had been at sea on July 20, and was within four miles of the spot where Ronald Platt's body had been dredged up.

When confronted with this information Albert Walker admitted that he and Platt had been out on his boat on July 20. He claimed Platt tripped, gashed his head, and fell over-board. There was nothing in the existing evidence to refute this account and investigators feared they would not be able to prove their case. But then they remembered that the fishermen told them about the ten-pound anchor found with the body. If they could find the anchor they might be able to prove that it was used to weigh Platt's body down, which would provide conclusive evidence against Albert Walker.

In searching sales records from the area, police found that Albert Walker (using the alias Ronald Platt) had purchased a ten-pound anchor. Eventually the anchor found with the body was traced and it was taken to the Forensic Sciences Centre.

Analysts determined that the anchor was almost brand new—a fact which jibed with evidence that Walker had purchased it just before July 20. It was made of galvanized steel and in some of the indentations of this steel police found leather fibers. These fibers matched the fibers found on the victim's belt. This belt also had a nick in the buckle. Using gas chromatography investigators determined that there was a microscopic amount of zinc in this nick. Zinc is used in the manufacture of galvanized steel. Investigators could now reasonably surmise that the belt and the anchor had been in contact extensive enough to deposit this trace evidence. They believed that Albert Walker tied the anchor to the victim's belt, dumped him overboard and assumed he'd never be found. They speculated that the anchor and the belt became unattached when the body was dredged up from the ocean floor.

To prove this theory they took a matching belt, put it on a dummy that matched the height and weight of the victim, and threaded the belt through the clasp-hole of a matching anchor. They found that this would have caused the buckle to rub up on the anchor at about the same spot the trace of zinc was discovered. The anchor would also dangle at an angle that would have produced the bruising on the victim's leg.

Albert Walker was charged with first-degree murder. Prosecutors presented the following scenario: Walker was on the lam from Canadian authorities; he moved to England to avoid prosecution; he hired Elaine Boyes to launder his stolen Canadian money; he got to know Ronald Platt and offered to finance his trip to Canada in order to assume Platt's identity; upon Platt's return to England Walker realized he would be exposed, so he decided he had to eliminate Platt; he coaxed him on to the boat, struck him in the head, threaded his belt through the anchor and threw him overboard.

After an eleven-day trial, Albert Walker was found guilty and sentenced in England to life in prison.

This case played much bigger in England and in Canada than it did in the U. S. Two books have been written on this case, as well as play that ran on London's West End. There was talk at one time of making it into a movie. We found out about it while researching another case in Canada. A reporter from the *Toronto Sun* told us to put "Rolex Man" into our search engine and all would become known to us. We did, and it did. Albert Walker presented a uniquely sinister, calculating character. His plan seemed virtually foolproof except that he had to plan on other people to make it work. Sadly for Walker, Ronald Platt was not the right person. Sad for Platt, too. On a related note, Walker was believed to have fathered two children with his own daughter, the woman neighbors described as subdued, and who went by the name "Sheena."

If you catch this episode it opens with an interview from John Copik, the fisherman who found the body. We had a devil of a time finding him; Devon, England, is far away from where we produce the show and we were doubtful he could ever be tracked down. Even the people who wrote books on the case had no idea where he was. But our producer set up shot in Devon for a couple of days, hung out at the local pubs and restaurants, and asked a lot of questions. One day Copik showed up while she was eating lunch. A gigantic man, with a bushy head of hair, he looked down at our producer and said in a thick, regional English accent, that if she had gone to all this trouble to find him he ought to at least introduce himself.

She explained who we were, they had a couple of pints and something to eat, and the next day he took her and our camera crew out to where he found the body. He gave us a spectacular interview—made all the better because he looks like he just stepped out of central casting. And the shots of Devon are absolutely beautiful.

Beautiful, however, is not what comes to mind in a story that amply illustrates that all Great Pretenders don't have to be upstanding citizens. In this story, which we called "Pastoral Care," the Pretender was a convict in the middle of a life term.

Green Haven state correctional facility is one of the toughest maximum security prisons in the country. Its walls—more than two feet thick—loom thirty feet above the ground. Another thirty feet are buried under the ground, making escape virtually impossible. The entire complex takes up one square mile. It's violent. It's overcrowded. And it's home to almost two thousand of New York state's most violent criminals, a quarter of whom are convicted murderers.

The year 1981 was the first year women were employed as corrections officers. There were fifty of them on staff—all brand new to the job. One of them was thirty-one-year-old Donna Payant, a mother of three children whose husband and father were both corrections officers at different facilities. Some of the older guards resented having women on staff, and after a couple of untoward incidents Donna filed, and later dropped, a sexual harassment suit against her supervisors.

On May 16, 1981, Donna didn't show up for the regular evening roll call. Prison officials instituted an emergency lockdown. All prisoners were confined to their cells while corrections officers combed the prison, room by room. But there was no sign of Donna Payant. Her car was in the lot and she hadn't punched her time card, so there was no explanation of her whereabouts.

The next morning prison officials got a call from workers at a nearby landfill. They said they had found the badly mutilated body of a blond female, in the uniform of a Green Haven corrections officer. She was soon identified as Donna Payant, the first female corrections officer to die in U.S. history to die in the line of duty.

She was found with ligatures around her neck and wrists, had been sexually violated and strangled to death. The first question was how had she ended up in the landfill. And the answer seemed to be that whoever killed her was someone inside the prison. He had apparently been able to get the body into one of the prison's trash receptacles without being seen by anyone. That would not be an easy thing to do, and it led to speculation that perhaps the killer was a fellow corrections officer. This seemed to make sense. Donna had made enemies with her sexual harassment suit, and few prisoners would be so unsupervised that they could get her alone, rape her, kill her, and get her into the trash without being detected.

Donna's death was big news and officials were under intense pressure to find her killer. They set up a task force inside the prison and interviewed everyone who might have had contact with her on the day of her murder. Guards were the primary focus of the investigation, until an unusual piece of evidence was uncovered during Donna's autopsy.

She was found to have what appeared to be bite marks on her chest, which indicated that the killer probably had a history of sexual assault. In fact, because of the bite mark Donna's murder was soon characterized as a "signature killing." Forensic psychologists said whoever killed her—and bit her—had almost certainly done this sort of thing before, and that the bite mark was a "signature" the killer would be compelled to leave on his victim. The investigation now turned to the inmates. Were there any among the Green Haven's more than five hundred convicted killers who had raped and bitten his victims?

The task force went through the records of all the sex-killers in the prison population, which was no small task. In the meantime they sent a copy of the bite marks from Donna Payant's body to a well-known forensic ondontologist, Dr. Lowell Levine. He took one look at the mark and said he recognized it immediately. It looked exactly like a photograph he used in lectures to criminology students. And it belonged to signature sex-killer named Lemuel Smith. Levine didn't even know where Lemuel Smith was incarcerated. But he called up officials at Green Haven and said he wanted to venture a guess. Did they have an inmate named Lemuel Smith, and if so, would Smith have had any contact with Donna Payant?

The answer to both questions was yes. Lemuel Smith was serving life for the rape/murder of two women, both of whom had been strangled with ligatures and bitten. But Smith was considered a model prisoner; in fact, he was a chaplain's aide with a perfect record.

As for Donna Payant and Lemuel Smith knowing each other, the answer was yes to this question as well. The two had established something of a friendship, one made possible by the remarkably free access Lemuel was given because of his position as a chaplain's aide.

A closer examination of Lemuel's record, which, for some reason, had not happened before Donna Payant's murder, turned up an alarming bit of news. Four years earlier, Dr. Zvi Klopott, a psychiatrist, had diagnosed Lemuel Smith as a paranoid schizophrenic with a borderline personality disorder. Dr. Klopott's report was remarkably clear: He said that Smith was delusional, had a distorted sense of reality, and that without constant psychiatric care was certain to kill again.

Still, there were a host of unanswered questions, the first being how would Smith get the privacy needed to kill Donna and dispose of the body. Detectives converged on the chaplain's office. It had recently been cleaned, and a painstaking examination turned up three hairs that were later found to be microscopically consistent with Donna Payant's.

This was circumstantial evidence at best. Donna was known to frequent the chaplain's office and her hairs being there did not necessarily implicate Lemuel Smith in her murder. For definitive proof investigators would have to turn to the bite marks on Donna's body. One mark was clear and highly distinctive. In an almost perfect crescent created by the lower teeth there was a large space—the biter was either missing his lower right incisor or there was a large space between his front bottom teeth and the incisor.

The mark was compared to a mark taken from one of Lemuel Smith's previous victims. Dr. Levine made slides of both marks and superimposed them on top of each other. There was no question that the bite marks were remarkably similar. Most people in the forensic community considered this to be an almost perfect "match." The marks on both victims were clear, and Lemuel Smith had unique dentition, which made for a distinctive mark in both samples.

Now some of Donna's unusual behavior on the day of her murder began to make sense. Prosecutors believed that Smith used the telephone in the chaplain's office to call Donna Payant He had made a jewelry box for Donna, which he wanted to give to her as a gift. A personal call from an inmate would have been an embarrassment for an inexperienced guard like Donna, and she stormed into the chaplain's office. Once there, the two may have argued, or perhaps Donna rejected Smith or his gift. Infuriated, Smith attacked Donna; he sexually assaulted her, strangled her, and at some point, bit her. Given his status as a model inmate he was able to wrap her body and put it in the dumpster without being seen.

What made the story even more tragic was this was the exact scenario predicted by the psychiatrist, Dr. Klopott. He said Lemuel Smith would often fantasize of having relationships with female acquaintances. If they rejected him—or even slighted him—in any way the fantasy would fall apart and he would become so enraged he would revert to an almost child-like state of rage. His previous two victims were both women he had befriended before killing. Dr. Klopott's report was explicit that Lemuel Smith should never have unrestricted contact with any female. Instead, he was considered a model prisoner and given almost free run of the prison.

Lemuel Smith was tried for the murder of Donna Payant, convicted in January 1983, and sentenced to death. That sentence later was overturned on constitutional grounds. He continues to deny he was involved in the crime, stating that the wound which was a key element in his conviction wasn't a bite mark at all, but an injury caused by the trash compactor and bulldozer in the landfill. He insists he was framed by prison guards, who were known to sell drugs to inmates and even provide prostitutes for them. For investigators, however, there is no question: Lemuel Smith had the means and the opportunity to kill Donna Payant, a contention which is supported by the bite mark found on her body.

Today Lemuel Smith spends twenty-three hours a day in solitary confinement and has no unrestricted access to anyone.

The State of New York gave *Forensic Files* some restricted access to Lemuel Smith and a lot of it is in the episode. The producer described it as one of the strangest and scariest experiences of his career.

Smith is a huge man, well over six feet tall, and well over two hundred pounds. Prison guards did their best to make sure that he was not alone with anyone in the *Forensic Files* crew, even for a second. But prison construction has a logic all its own and it made for a strange encounter when we met Lemuel.

Prisons are made of locked-off areas; some, like the living quarters, can be the size of football fields. Others can be the size of a closet or a small office. The idea is that if something happens the problem area can be locked off and contained until help arrives. Before our interview with Lemuel the crew had set up the camera and lights in a secure area down the hall from the maximum-security lockup. The idea was to have the camera ready as soon as Lemuel arrived; prison authorities were only giving us an hour and we had to be ready.

Our producer was in an adjoining room waiting to meet Lemuel and bring him in. A prison guard introduced Lemuel to our producer and then, to the producer's considerable surprise, left the two of them alone while he opened the adjoining room—the one in which we planned to do the interview. This is not a quick process. The opening and closing of heavy locked doors takes time and moves even more slowly because one room has to be completely locked down before the next room is opened. This left Lemuel and our producer in the same small, locked-down room for about five minutes while they waited to be led to the room with the camera equipment.

While Lemuel seemed harmless enough—and even charming—our producer, who had interviewed Lemuel's psychiatrist and was familiar with his past, said he couldn't help think how unusual it was to be locked down with a guy who was capable of the kinds of murderous rages that had left a number of people dead. He said later that he thought it best to just make small talk and not discuss Lemuel's case until they got to the interview room, where the corrections officer was waiting.

The problem was, what do you say to a man who has spent more than two decades in solitary confinement? "How's the food?" "Do you like it here?" Luckily, the producer came armed with two cartons of cigarettes, which Lemuel refused, saying he quit smoking years earlier. But it was enough to break the ice, and enough to get them to the interview room without incident.

And it was a good thing because the interview became a bit contentious. It's not at all uncommon for an interviewer to have to play "devil's advocate." In other words he or she has to present a worst-case scenario or present a set of facts that the interviewee does not agree with, and often holds in open contempt. Such was the case with Lemuel. He was presented with the case against him—particularly the bite mark evidence—and he wasn't happy about it. Here's a part of the transcript.

Producer: "You can see the match. You're just saying the match is fabricated?"

Smith: "I can see it, everybody can see it. But it's not a bite mark. Here's the body, it gets put in a compactor, crushed all this is, but the only thing clear and distinct on it is the bite mark? Not unless it came afterward."

In other words, he was being framed by prison guards. It's a charge that held water for some time with local media and Donna Payant's family. They claimed that Donna had made a lot of enemies by standing up for her rights, and by threatening to expose an old-boy network in which corrections officers made money on the side by providing drugs and sometimes women to inmates. Those allegations were ultimately put to rest—at least as far as the media were concerned—by the local District Attorney's office, but the rumors about a cover-up persist to this day. Which is another thing that irritates Lemuel Smith. He says has nothing to lose by telling the truth. After all, he's already serving two life terms for killing women before he even met Donna Payant.

Producer: "Are you bitter?"

Lemuel: "Bitter? I'm angry but I'm not bitter. What I'm angry at is the correction officers that turned on me, the correction officers that we'd been together for years laughed and joked together, when it come time to trial right, they're up there, you're saying that and this—saying you gotta be calm, you gotta be calm, be calm. How you gonna be calm when somebody lying on you? I want to split their face. Somebody sitting up there deliberately lying on you. Deliberately trying to put you in the electric chair, for what? To save the name of

Department of Corrections. And that's the way they play the game."

As our producer later told it, when a two-hundred-fifty-pound man who's in prison for three brutal murders gets his temper up it tends to get your attention—especially when he's only three feet way. Some of that exchange is in the on-air episode and Lemuel's rage is clearly apparent.

Forensic Files talks to a lot of criminal profilers. Their job is to assess a crime scene and try to figure out what type of person committed the crime, and possibly predict his future behavior. Lemuel Smith was one of the few times when we've talked to a psychiatrist, Dr. Klopott, who could tell us essentially how a murderer is made. As a result, Lemuel's story provides an unusual—and rare—insight into the mind of a killer.

He was the highly intelligent son of a fundamentalist preacher. Shortly before he was born, an elder brother, John, died in infancy. His mother, apparently, never recovered from the loss, despite hoping that Lemuel would be able fill the void. According to Dr. Klopott, this had a devastating effect on Lemuel's early development. Here's part of our interview that we had to cut from the final program.

Dr. Klopott: "She was a loving mother, but for Lemuel it felt that something was missing and he blamed his brother John for that. What he did was what some kids do when the situation is impossible: they convert the situation. It's a process called a reactive formation. What he did was he took that dead brother and made him part of himself. He didn't sit around and say okay this is what I'm gonna do, but psychologically that's what happened. But he hated that brother."

Dr. Klopott says this accounts for why Lemuel was capable of unspeakable violence but was also considered a model prisoner. Placed in a situation where he got positive feedback and some semblance of affection he was calm, nonviolent and well-mannered. But if that affection were withdrawn the con-

Lemuel Smith. The space between his lower teeth would solve a murder investigation.

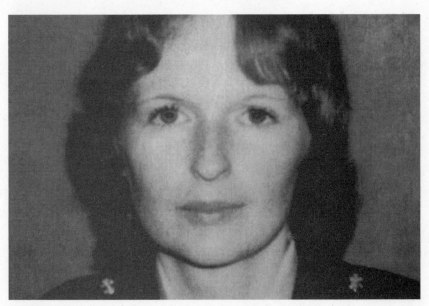

Donna Payant, the first female U.S. corrections officer to die in the line of duty.

Lemuel Smith being interviewed by *Forensic Files*. He still maintains his innocence.

sequences were explosive.

Dr. Klopott. "Whenever a situation arises when he feels unloved, or unattended to, brother John comes out and says "don't worry I'll take care of business." And then Lemuel—that part of his personality that's nice and pleasant takes a back seat or hides out in a corner someplace while brother John takes care of the anger."

And that's what happened with Donna Payant. When she rejected the jewelry box Lemuel had made for her he reverted to an almost childlike state of rage—exactly what Dr. Klopott had predicted would happen. It's tragic to realize that Donna Payant's murder could have been prevented, but perhaps even more frightening to realize that Lemuel's behavior could have been predicted with such uncanny accuracy.

While even murders can be predicted, some criminal behavior

is so bizarre it's impossible to anticipate. Take a story we enti-tled "Bad Blood."

The tiny town of Kipling, Saskatchewan, is nestled along Canada's pristine southwestern prairies. The town is so small that farm animals outnumber residents. Dr. John Schneeberg-er came to Kipling in 1987 from South Africa. He became a well-respected doctor, looked up to by residents who appreci-ated his youth, his candor, and his willingness to help.

Dr. Schneeberger was on duty the night a young woman named Candy came to the Kipling hospital after a heated argu-ment with her boyfriend. She was so upset she wanted some medications to calm her down, so she sought out Dr. Schnee-berger, whom she knew well: he was her regular doctor and two years earlier had delivered her baby.

Instead of some pills Dr. Schneeberger recommended an injection. This surprised Candy, but she trusted the doctor and consented. Almost immediately she went numb and became disoriented. She never went completely unconscious but she was unable to control her body and her memory was sketchy. Hours later, after she regained complete control of her facul-ties, she came to believe that Dr. Schneeberger had raped her after giving her the shot. She was so sure of this that she decid-ed to take of her underwear and place it in an airtight bag before leaving the hospital.

The next day she went to a rape crisis center where she had the contents of the bag analyzed and also submitted to a rape kit test on herself. Her underwear was found to contain semen, as was a vaginal swab from the rape kit. Blood tests also revealed a drug—called Versed—in her system. Versed is a pre-anesthetic, used to prepare patients for major surgery. Candy knew she had not had sex with anyone the previous night—at least consensually—and also had no access to a drug like Versed. For her, the results confirmed what she suspected: that Dr. Schneeberger had drugged her and then raped her.

She came forward with charges against him. But no one—even some of her friends and family—believed her. Dr. Schneeberger was a respected member of the community with a spotless record. People assumed Candy had ulterior motives. Perhaps, they thought, she was romantically interested in the doctor and was getting revenge for having her advances spurned. Or perhaps she was using a trumped-up charge to seek some sort of out of court financial settlement.

For his part, Dr. Schneeberger steadfastly maintained his innocence. In fact, he was so willing to clear his name that he told local authorities that he would be more than happy to submit to a DNA test. If his DNA didn't match the profile taken from Candy's underwear and vaginal swab that would be proof of his innocence. When the comparisons were finally done it was just as the doctor predicted: the profiles didn't match. He wasn't charged, was allowed to continue practicing medicine, and Candy's reputation took a savage beating.

Yet she stuck to her story. She told anyone and everyone that she was absolutely convinced she'd been raped by Dr. Schneeberger, and that something—she didn't know what—had transpired to create a false reading on the DNA test. Her unwillingness to let the case go began to create difficulties for Dr. Schneeberger, so almost a year later he submitted to a second DNA test. This time around his blood was drawn by a registered nurse—in the presence of police, who then maintained a chain of custody by transporting the blood vials to their forensic laboratory.

Again, there was no match. Dr. Schneeberger was cleared, and told reporters he had a theory about Candy's story. He said he had given Candy a shot of Versed on the night she came to the hospital. She was highly agitated and he thought this was necessary to calm her down. He explained that Versed is known to cause erotic hallucinations and thought this might account for her absolute conviction that she'd been sexually assaulted.

He had no explanation for the semen found in the rape kit, but since it wasn't his DNA his involvement in the case appeared to be over. In 1994, the investigation into Candy's rape allegations was officially closed.

That, however, wasn't good enough for Candy. She decided to conduct her own investigation and hired a private investigator. Not bound by normal rules of police conduct, the investigator broke into Dr. Schneeberger's car and found a capsule of lip balm. This, he knew, was likely to be a rich source of DNA; epithelial cells from the user's lips would be preserved within the lip balm. The capsule was taken and tested. And Candy got her first piece of positive news: The DNA profile from the lip balm matched the profile from the semen found in her underwear.

But there were problems. First, there was no way to prove the epithelial cells on the lip balm belonged to Dr. Schneeberger. Second, the evidence—even if it implicated the doctor—couldn't be used in court because it had been obtained illegally. Candy took the only option available to her. She did an end-run around the criminal justice system and filed a civil suit.

The doctor, professing weariness at these repeated assaults on his reputation, said he would agree to one last DNA test. This time the procedure was conducted at the police forensics lab and was videotaped. In the tape the technician wants to take blood from the doctor's finger. The doctor refuses, saying he has a disease that would cause his hands to bruise and, since the test was voluntary, the technician is unable to force the doctor to do anything he doesn't want to.

The technician inserts a needle into the doctor's left arm. Nothing comes out. She tries a number of times and is eventually able to extract a sample. She can be heard on the tape saying that the blood "doesn't look fresh." When the sample was sent for testing analysts said the blood was too degraded to extract a DNA profile, which meant either that the doctor had old blood running in his veins or that something had happened while the blood was being drawn. Still, officials were hesitant to move forward. The doctor had passed two previous DNA tests, and had no prior record of sexual assault.

While Canadian law enforcement decided what to do there was a stunning development. Dr. Schneeberger's own stepdaughter claimed he had sexually assaulted her. The fourteen-year-old's story was remarkably like Candy's. She said that for years the doctor had been sneaking into her room and given her injections before assaulting her. The girl told her mother, who searched the doctor's home office and found a box of condoms, some syringes, and a large amount of . . . Versed.

His wife went to the authorities and the doctor was ordered to undergo yet another round of DNA tests. Again the procedure was videotaped. Technicians took several blood samples, from his finger, not his arm; they also took samples of his hair and saliva.

This time the DNA profiles matched the samples taken from Candy's rape kit. Incredibly, seven years had passed since the rape and, finally, she had proof that the good doctor was anything but good—he was a rapist who used his privileged position to assault her, his stepdaughter and perhaps any number of other women who were afraid to come forward.

The question now was how had Dr. Schneeberger fooled three previous DNA tests, especially since a nurse and police witnessed the blood being drawn. On the stand, he finally told the story. He said he had surgically implanted a plastic tube under the skin of his left arm and filled the tube with blood from one of his patients. That is why he always insisted the blood be drawn from his left arm. Since the first two rounds of DNA testing were done within a year of the rape the blood remained fresh and didn't arouse any suspicions. By the time

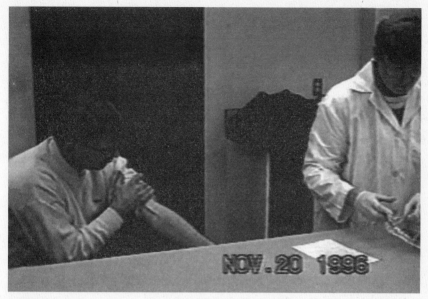

Evidence video of Dr. Schneeberger's blood test. Note the bulge in his arm. His ruse worked for years, but Candy's persistence finally revealed the truth.

of the third round of testing, five years had passed and the blood had degraded so much it was barely even liquid. Yet it was enough to keep the authorities away. If Dr. Schneeberger had not violated his own stepdaughter, he might never have been charged in Candy's rape.

He was found guilty, sentenced to six years in prison, and had his medical license suspended.

A person could read this story over and over again and never truly appreciate what happened. The videotape of the "fake" blood being drawn from the good doctor's arm simply must be seen. He is coy, charming, and unflappable. When the nurse tries to get blood from his finger, he calmly waves her off and directs her to his left arm. You would never know anything was amiss—that is, until you see how much difficulty the nurse has performing a simple procedure like drawing blood.

Thanks to modern television technology we enhanced the video and zoomed in on the spot where the needle is injected into the doctor's arm. A close examination—blown-up and in slow motion—clearly reveals the plastic tube. At first, it appears to be an audacious move on the doctor's part, but then you realize it's not so much audacity as sheer desperation. Candy was not going to let up and he had to devise some way to counter her charges. He hoped that by manipulating the science he could get away with her rape, but Candy's unflagging determination to get to the truth finally revealed what many authorities have described as one of the most elaborate ruses in criminal history.

As for Candy, perhaps it's best to let her have the last word on Dr. Schneeberger. Here's part of her interview that didn't make the final cut of the program.

"He's such a sick man. How can he pretend to be so normal, and also have this really dark side? What the hell happened in his childhood? You know, you can't always blame everything on everybody's childhood. But what happened to make him such a twisted person? And why me? What did I do? He does have a side of him that—it's hard to believe he was a good doctor. He was just a really bad person."

While we were interviewing Candy she got a call telling her that Dr. Schneeberger's parole had been denied. Her reaction is caught on camera. She spent seven long years of her life making sure he was brought to justice, and is not shy about celebrating the fact that he was going to remain behind bars for just a little while longer.

SIX
Healers or Killers?

As a doctor, John Schneeberger brings certain advantages to the table that most criminals don't have. Doctors are well-educated, particularly about the sciences, they have access to a variety of drugs, they know a lot about how the human body works, and they work in a job that commands respect. From a position like that a person could help a lot of people. He could also, if he were so inclined, hurt people—and be better equipped than most people to get away with it.

For some doctors the age-old dictum, "above all, do no harm," is nothing more than a saying. *Forensic Files* has done a surprising number of stories in which doctors and other members of the health-care professions have gotten up to no good. Greed, lust, envy, ambition—all the things that motivate murderers, aren't lost on doctors with compulsion to kill. Their plans are sometimes more elaborate, but sometimes it's the complexity of those plans that lands them in jail.

Here's a case we called "Foundation of Lies."

On January 1, 1990, friends of Noreen Boyle reported that she had been missing for the past twenty-four hours. Noreen was the wife of Dr. John Boyle, a prominent osteopath, in Mansfield, Ohio. Rumors about her disappearance quickly surfaced in the quiet, tightly-knit community. Many felt that Noreen may have just walked out on her life; others said she would never leave her children. What wasn't in dispute was that she had recently filed for divorce.

Some speculated that she may have been in trouble with the law. Eleven months prior to Noreen's disappearance, she had adopted a two-year-old Taiwanese girl, whom she named Elizabeth. Many viewed her adoption as irregular; they had heard that Noreen bypassed normal channels and simply bought her daughter. One rumor had it that Noreen had told her brother-in-law, C.J. Boyle, that she had purchased Elizabeth for five-thousand dollars from the little girl's mother.

Elizabeth's mother was unmarried, and her father was deceased. United States immigration laws allow for the adoption of foreign children whose parents are dead or whose parents have abandoned them. Children with one parent can be adopted if that parent shows that he or she cannot take care of the child. A man who had worked with Christian missionaries in Taiwan believed that Elizabeth's mother was coerced into signing the adoption papers.

A few people believed that the adoption of Elizabeth was a "test-run" for a black market baby adoption ring that Noreen had hoped to create.

Police had no clues to her whereabouts, and for them the rumors were just that—rumors. They took the investigation down the old-fashioned route and decided to "look at the in-laws before they looked at the outlaws." Investigators soon learned that Dr. Boyle had had numerous affairs during his twenty-year marriage. His wife was apparently willing to look the other way in order to provide stability for their children. But then she found out about Dr. Boyle's latest mistress, Sherri Campbell. Noreen told friends and family she was divorcing Dr. Boyle because she learned that Sherri was pregnant.

Meanwhile, police followed Dr. Boyle, who was in the process of moving to his new home in Erie, Pennsylvania. On January 4, he was observed buying a green indoor-outdoor carpet. Credit-card receipts also indicated that he rented a jack-hammer over the New Year holiday. Investigators found nothing unusual in his actions at that time. But they did find something unusual in the story told to them by the real estate agent who had sold the house.

Dr. Boyle introduced Sherri as his "wife." The house they looked at was $299,000, and Dr. Boyle agreed to pay the full price if the current owners could be out by December 30. He also asked the real estate agent what kind of floor was in the basement. She assumed that he had plans to lower the basement. The "Boyles" signed a tentative agreement of sale, and Sherri signed her name, S. Noreen Boyle.

On January 18, 1990—almost three weeks after Noreen's disappearance—the Boyle's son, Collier, gave his formal statement to police. He claimed that on the night of December 31, he heard his parents having a loud argument. Following a heated exchange, he heard a thump, as if someone had been hit. The following day, the Boyle's three-year-old daughter, Elizabeth, gave what little description she could of what happened that night, and it appeared to corroborate her brother's story.

After hearing the children's testimony, police believed Noreen had been attacked, and probably killed, by her husband. The motive? One of the oldest and most common. Police believed that Noreen was murdered so Dr. Boyle would not have to pay alimony and child support. He wanted to start a new life with his new family and wanted Noreen out of the way.

On January 25, police searched Dr. Boyle's new home. They went to the basement, and saw the green carpet that he was observed buying on January 4. On top of the carpet were some newly constructed shelves. Police moved the shelves and lifted the carpet. Underneath was a spongy area of wet cement.

Slowly, by hand, the investigators dug through the cement to find what was believed to be the body of Noreen Boyle. Dental records later confirmed that it was her body that was found in the basement. Cause of death was determined to be strangulation with blunt force trauma to the head as a contributory factor.

To many, it was obvious who had killed Noreen Boyle, but the condition of the body left the forensic examiners with limited physical evidence. In addition, the rumors that Noreen had perhaps made enemies by her "irregular" adoption of little Elizabeth were persistent, and could conceivably provide a jury with reasonable doubt if Dr. Boyle were eventually brought to trial.

On January 28, Mark Davis, a friend of Dr. Boyle's, had returned to his Mansfield, Ohio, home after vacationing in Mexico. In his yard he had found a large pile of concrete. He called the police who came and took the concrete as evidence. This concrete was rough, and it appeared it had recently been broken into pieces. The edges were sharp and had not been worn down by the elements.

Police thought it was possible that the cement in Mark Davis's yard was the original cement from Dr. Boyle's new basement. To find out they contacted Larry Pishtelli, a forensic engineer known for doing unusual analyses of this type. Pishtelli was handed four bags of cement. One bag contained cement recovered by Mark Davis. Two bags contained cement from Noreen Boyle's tomb. The last bag contained pieces of cement taken from the original floor of Dr. Boyle's new home.

Pishtelli took small pieces from each bag. He then sliced the samples with a saw and polished the newly cut surfaces. Then he examined each of the pieces microscopically. Cement can become distinguishable by its mineralogical make-up and the concentration of air voids, which are essentially air bubbles created when the cement is poured. The mixture of materials will affect the weight of the cement and the size and number of air voids. Cement taken from a common area would have the same percentage of air voids.

Through this system and the mineralogical make-up of the cement, Pishtelli concluded that the cement in Mark Davis's yard came from the basement floor of Dr. Boyle's new home. No one but Dr. Boyle had a reason to remove this cement, no one but Dr. Boyle had a connection between his home and Mark Davis's property. There was no plausible reason to dig up that section of the basement—except to conceal a body. When questions about Elizabeth's adoption were put to rest it was clear there was only one person with a motive to kill Noreen Boyle—her husband, John Boyle. He was found guilty and given a sentence of life without the possibility of parole for twenty years. But the story does not end there.

Despite the evidence, speculation about the murder persisted, and Dr. Boyle steadfastly maintained his innocence. He insisted that the body in the basement was not Noreen's. There were discrepancies in the autopsy report. The corpse was measured at five-feet four-and-one-half inches, and Noreen was five-foot-six. Also, the weight was off by at least thirty pounds, and the eye color was incorrectly identified.

Years went by until Noreen Boyle's son, Collier, agreed to an examination of his mother. On June 12, 1995, Noreen's body was exhumed from a Baltimore, Maryland, cemetery. Mansfield's chief laboratory scientist, Tony Tamborosco, drew blood from Noreen's sister for a mitochondrial DNA analysis.

Mitochondrial DNA can be found outside of the cell nucleus, and is normally used in cases where body samples have become old and degraded. It's not as good as "nuclear" DNA, but in the absence of traditional testing it is surprisingly accurate. All mitochondrial DNA is passed maternally. When scientists compare the mitochondrial DNA of the deceased with that of a family member, they can determine if the two are related because they would share their mother's mitochondria.

The mitochondrial DNA from Noreen Boyle's family and the exhumed corpse matched. But to eliminate any doubt officials had the skeletal remains analyzed by Douglas Owsley of the Smithsonian Institution Skeletal Institute. He compared Noreen Boyle's dental records with the remains of the skeleton. He determined that the remains were indeed those Noreen Boyle's. The discrepancies in the death report were found to be errors made by a poorly trained pathologist. Noreen was laid to rest once and for all. Her husband remains behind bars.

Increasingly, law enforcement outfits around the country are using video recording technology as part of their investigations. This is proving invaluable in court but it's also a godsend if you're producing a television program In this case police, concerned that there be no margin for error when they checked to see what was in Dr. Boyle's new basement, recorded everything. As a result, the moment in which Noreen Boyle's body is found is caught on tape, and to use the words of one of the detectives who was present, the scene was "surreal." If you watch this episode, most of it is there.

The cement is still wet and when her body is exhumed it almost bursts out of the ground. More than one person has said it resembles a birth. Once free from its cement grave the body practically rockets to the surface. The discovery spelled the end for Dr. Boyle, although he didn't realize it at the time. By all accounts he remained convinced that police simply could not outsmart him. To the end—even after his conviction—he thought his plan would work. The odd thing is that all the investigators on the case described it as one of the clumsiest attempts to cover up a murder that they'd ever seen. There was no one else with a plausible motive, Noreen was far too high-profile to be able to disappear without a trace. She wasn't the type of person who normally falls victim to random violence, and there was a string of Dr. Boyle's former paramours who were ready and willing to testify about his contempt for his wife.

His practice was so successful that one in every thirteen residents of Mansfield used him as their physician. If he'd just consented to the divorce, agreed to a settlement and child support payments, he would have recouped his losses fairly quickly. In any event, he had the resources to live in extraordinary luxury even after a hefty divorce payout. Now he's in a prison lockdown and, if he behaves himself behind bars, will get out around the time he could have been settling into a comfortable retirement.

The same could not be said for a medical student in North Carolina who was days from being certified as a doctor when he was charged with first-degree murder. But you'd never get a hint of that from our title for the story. We called it "Letter Perfect" because it featured a brand new field of crime science—forensic linguistics.

On an April morning in 1992, an emergency medical team in Raleigh, North Carolina, responded to a call from a suburban apartment building. They entered to find a young man in his bed. He looked like he was sleeping, but paramedics quickly discovered he was dead.

The deceased was twenty-three-year-old Michael Hunter, a computer programmer and recent college graduate. The roommate who found his body said he went to wake Hunter up and found him unresponsive. There was no sign of trauma, and the room was in perfect order. The report written up at the scene by paramedics stated that Hunter "appeared to have gone to sleep and never woke up." Since he was young and in apparently perfect health this didn't make sense.

Two days after his death an autopsy was performed. Pathologists found an injection mark on the inside of Hunter's left arm. Thinking this might have something to do with what killed him, they ordered an extensive toxicological workup. The tests revealed that Hunter had normal doses of two over-the-counter cold medicines in his system. He also had a lethal dose of Lidocaine.

This also didn't make sense. Lidocaine is a local anesthetic used most often as a numbing agent. But it's also used in emergency medical situations in which paramedics need to stabilize heartbeat. When injected it works quickly and can mean the difference between life and death for a heart attack victim who is being rushed to the hospital.

But why would Michael Hunter have Lidocaine in his system—in lethal amounts? At first, pathologists thought it might have been injected by the paramedics who were first on the scene. But their on-site reports stated clearly that Hunter was dead when they arrived, and that no drugs were administered to him.

The official cause of death was now Lidocaine poisoning. But this raised more questions that it answered. Where had Hunter gotten the Lidocaine, a controlled substance. Had he given himself the injection or had someone done it for him? Was his death a suicide . . . or a murder?

Police started asking the obvious question: Was there anyone who wanted to kill Michael Hunter? They soon found that Hunter was involved in what even he had described as an "unconventional" living arrangement. He shared an apartment with Joseph Mannino, a twenty-six-year-old medical student, and Garry Walston, a thirty-year-old landscape architect. The three were unofficially "married," and had exchanged rings and pledged their loyalty to each other a year earlier.

But, as in many love triangles, things hadn't worked out as planned. Garry Walston told investigators that Hunter and Mannino had grown apart, and had not only fallen out of love, they'd begun to hate each other. The situation became so untenable that Garry was faced with the unenviable task of having to choose between Hunter and Mannino. He chose Hunter, and soon Mannino found himself the odd man out, relegated to a guest bedroom while he looked for another place to live.

This looked like motive to investigators. If Hunter were out of the way, Mannino would be free to resume his relationship with Garry Walston. As a medical student Mannino had access to Lidocaine and knew how to use it. And he was the person who found the body and called 911. When questioned, however, Mannino absolutely denied having anything to do with Hunter's death. He said he loved him and would never harm him.

For police, there was a big problem: no murder weapon and no witnesses. But Mannino was their only plausible suspect and they kept after him for days, and then weeks. When confronted with the fact that he appeared to have a motive to want Hunter dead, Mannino told police a strange story.

He said that Hunter had a history of debilitating migraine headaches, and that on the night of his death he had given him an injection of Lidocaine to help ease his pain. But it was a small dose, and not nearly enough to kill him. When investigators, thrown off by this admission, wanted to know why Mannino hadn't divulged this information earlier he had a perfectly reasonable explanation. Since he wasn't officially certified as a doctor his medical career would have been put in jeopardy if were found to have given someone an injection.

Mannino said it was possible that Hunter had killed himself. He knew where the Lidocaine was kept, knew how to administer it and, according to Mannino, had just found out that he was HIV positive and had talked about committing suicide rather than dying of AIDS. This didn't make sense to medical investigators on the case. They told police that if Hunter had given himself a lethal injection of Lidocaine it would have killed him so quickly that the needle would most likely still be in his arm or, at the least, somewhere in the room. They said the evidence at the scene indicated without a doubt that someone other than Hunter had administered the fatal injection.

Police were starting to close in on Joseph Mannino when the case went in an unexpected direction. Mannino said he found a computer disk in Hunter's possessions which contained suicide letters to his family and to himself and Garry Walston. There were no printed-out copies of the letters—all police had was the disk and the text, which meant there was no handwriting or ink to analyze. They didn't believe the letters were legitimate but needed a way to prove it.

They checked out the nearby North Carolina State University and found that there was a linguistics professor on staff, Dr. Carole Chaski, who was experimenting in the new field of forensic linguistics. Linguistics is basically the study of how people communicate in writing; not so much what they say when writing, but how they say it. Forensic linguistics had been used, with mixed success, to attempt to determine the real author of a sonnet attributed to Shakespeare as well as a number of other documents whose authorship was in question.

Dr. Chaski asked Michael Hunter's family to give him samples of his writing. Police obtained samples from Joseph Mannino. Dr. Chaski wanted to compare the writing structure in these documents to the writing structure in the suicide letters. To do this she used a computer program that broke all of the documents down word by word. The program then rebuilt each phrase in each document and analyzed how different parts of grammar—nouns, verbs, adjectives, adverbs—were used in relation to each other.

In the alleged suicide notes Dr. Chaski found that conjunctions such as "and" were used not so much to combine phrases, but large sentences. This was distinctive. The notes also contained an unusual use of adverbs. Instead of using just one adverb the author of the suicide letters tended to combine, or amplify them, using phrases like "very, very," or "never even."

This was also distinctive. And it never appeared in any of Michael Hunter's writing samples. It did, however, appear repeatedly in Joseph Mannino's writing, as did the unusual use of conjunctions. Dr. Chaski told police she was sure who wrote the suicide letters: Joseph Mannino, and he was still alive and well.

Police now had not only motive and opportunity on Mannino's part, they had proof that he was creating false evidence to cover up the crime. Their theory of the case was the Mannino waited to commit the murder until Garry Walston was out of town on business. When Michael Hunter went to sleep Mannino sneaked into his room and delivered the fatal injection, something doctors said could be done without waking the victim as long as the person handling the needle knew what he was doing.

Joseph Mannino was found guilty of involuntary manslaughter. The jury found it impossible to determine whether Michael Hunter had agreed to the Lidocaine injection. Mannino was sentenced to seven years and will never again be allowed to practice medicine.

In the wake of Michael Hunter's murder his mother had about as tough a year as anyone could have. Shortly after his death she found out she had breast cancer. The news that Michael was gay came as a complete surprise and had a devastating effect on his father. Upset, confused, and wanting to take justice into his own hands, he began drinking heavily and spiraled downward into a debilitating depression. Just before the trial began he came home in an alcoholic rage, put a gun to his head and killed himself while his horrified wife sat only a few feet away. For her, Joseph Mannino has not one, but two deaths on his hands.

Though she was as surprised as the rest of the family by Michael's sexual orientation she quickly accepted it and remains extremely close to Garry Walston, the man with whom her son planned to spend the rest of his life. The two spend holidays together and regularly visit Michael's grave, which is next to his father's in hillside cemetery in central North Carolina.

Joseph Mannino has faded from view. None of his other friends or fellow students know where he is. His story is its own tragedy. He came from a humble background, was highly intelligent, and was the first person in his family to go to college, where he did so well it seemed his future as a successful doctor was assured. Yet for someone with so much apparent brain power, the fake suicide letters are so contrived they're almost comical. How he thought a jury might buy the notes perhaps shows how desperate he was as investigators closed on him. Here's what Mannino has the victim, Michael Hunter, saying to his parents about his "HIV diagnosis" and subsequent decision to "commit suicide:"

"If you receive this note, then you know that I wanted to take my own life. I will use some medications I found in Joe's black bag. Please don't blame him for this because he doesn't know I have them, and because this is something I feel I have to do. It will also make it easier and hopefully painless. I have a close friend I have talked to about this, and who feel the same way I do. My friend is also willing to helm me with this, since I know Joe and Garry would never even think about helping me in this way."

Though some of the letter sounds almost preposterous, it's clear Mannino has at least considered the prospect that medical officials would conclude that without the help of another person Michael Hunter would have been found with a needle in his arm. When asked by police who this unnamed person was Mannino said he had no idea, which further convinced Garry Walston, the third person in the love triangle, that something was amiss. He knew all of Hunter's friends and coworkers and was positive someone would have told him if Hunter was contemplating suicide.

But the letter that caused the biggest problem and may have contributed greatly to the suicide of Michael Hunter's father was one that was never read in court and didn't make our program. As the investigation homed in on Joe Mannino he feared he would never be allowed to practice medicine, especially when it came out that he administered an injection without a license. He wrote a letter to Michael Hunter's parents asking them to assure authorities at the medical school that Michael's migraines were so painful that administering the injection was an act of kindness for which he should be forgiven. Not having the faintest idea that Mannino was the murderer, Hunter's parents did just that, and felt doubly betrayed when it was clear that Mannino's intentions in giving their son Lidocaine had nothing to do with kindness. By all accounts Hunter's father was livid beyond words that he had actually been duped into helping the person who killed his son.

From a TV perspective this was one of the most difficult cases we've ever done. Forensic linguistics is not the kind of thing that lends itself to television. It's cerebral, there's little in the way of physical evidence, and what little there is usually is nothing more than scraps of paper. To overcome this problem we pulled out the stops. Any viewer of this episode will notice sweeping camera moves that don't often appear in our program. We figured it was the only way we could make a forensic scientist sitting in front of a computer visually interesting. We also used a series of what are called lipstick cameras—small lenses about the thickness of a tube of lipstick (hence the name)—to make the documents themselves more visually dynamic. Finally, we had to do something to visualize the writing styles of the various players in the show. All we can say is, thank goodness for computer graphics and the people who know how to use them. Our post-production team came up with a way to show things like conjunctions and adverbs that was not only visually interesting—but made sense within the context of the actual case.

We were pleased with the final result; even more so after the forensic linguist herself, Dr. Chaski, called us to say she never thought her line of work could be made to "look" so compelling.

Another case in which a health-care worker turned from healer to killer is among the more tragic we've done, since the victims were young children. We called it "Nursery Crimes."

On Tuesday, August 24, 1982, Petti McCllelan took her fourteen month old daughter, Chelsea, to Dr. Kathy Holland's office. The youngster had a case of the sniffles. As Petti and the doctor were discussing Chelsea's medical history, the doctor's nurse offered to take Chelsea to another room to play.

Within five minutes, Chelsea's body had gone limp, and she was barely breathing; soon afterward she went into seizures. Dr. Holland and her nurse, Genene Jones, stabilized the child enough to transport her to nearby Sid Peterson Hospital.

Upon arrival, Chelsea was breathing on her own, and Petti McCllelan marveled at the efficiency of Dr. Holland and Nurse Jones. Doctors could offer no explanation for the sudden onset of the seizure, but Chelsea was born prematurely, and had a few isolated incidents of shallow breathing in the past.

Almost a month after that incident, Petti had returned to Dr. Holland with Chelsea and her son, Cameron, who had the flu. Dr. Holland also suggested that Chelsea be given a quick exam as a follow-up to the seizure episode. While Chelsea was there, Dr. Holland also ordered some childhood immunizations for her.

Chelsea was given one injection in her left thigh. Within moments, she began to have trouble breathing. Nurse Jones explained that she was just reacting to the pain of the injection. Then, nurse Jones proceeded to give Chelsea the other injection in her right thigh. By the time she pulled the syringe out, the child was not breathing at all. She had turned blue and began having a seizure. An ambulance was summoned, and Chelsea was on her way to Sid Peterson hospital again.

Hospital staff stabilized Chelsea, and she began to turn pink again. Dr. Holland decided that she wanted Chelsea transported to a San Antonio hospital, where she could get more specialized care. Dr. Holland hoped to find out the cause of these seizures. The emergency helicopter was unavailable, and the ICU was full, so they decided to send Chelsea to Santa Rosa by ambulance. Nurse Jones accompanied Chelsea on the ride, while Petti and her husband, Reid, followed in their car. When they had driven about eight miles, Chelsea started to go into arrest again. Dr. Holland, who was riding up front, came to the back. Chelsea was given drugs to restart her heart, but to no avail. About twenty minutes after arriving at the hospital, Chelsea was dead.

Her death was attributed to a seizure of undetermined origin.

Two more children were admitted to Sid Peterson Hospital under emergency circumstances in the next couple of weeks. On September 23, five-month-old Rolinda Ruff was taken to Dr. Holland because she had been suffering from intermittent diarrhea for the past thirteen days. Dr. Holland said that Rolinda was dehydrated, and asked Nurse Jones to administer some IV fluids.

It was just a matter of minutes before Rolinda was choking and unable to breathe. Again, a child left in Dr. Holland's care was taken to Sid Peterson under a "code blue." The emergency room staff stabilized her. But Dr. Frank Bradley, an anesthesiologist, realized that something was terribly wrong. His report stated that "the child was coming out from under Anectine."

Anectine is used to restrict muscle movement. It is primarily used in children, to aid in the insertion of breathing tubes. There would be no reason for this drug to have been administered to the child. Hospital administration decided to hold an emergency meeting, but in the meantime, there was yet another emergency.

A baby, Chris Parker, had come in for a routine exam. Shortly after being examined by Nurse Jones, he went into arrest. Dr. Holland was brought in, and she ordered two different drugs to ease the baby's distress. Somebody had noticed a half-filled syringe on the child's bed. It wasn't one of the needles the nurse had just used. Dr. Holland ordered the nurse to get rid of it.

At noon that day, Dr. Holland had an appointment with a hospital administrator, Tony Hall. He believed that the children had been given succinylcholine, the powerful relaxant sold as Anectine.

Dr. Holland tried to track down the usage of succinylcholine in her office. Three bottles had been ordered, but one was missing. One bottle was found that appeared to be full. But there were needle holes in the cap. Analysis indicated the bottles had actually been thinned out to make them look full.

Suspicion started to surround Dr. Holland's licensed vocational nurse, Genene Jones. A formal inquiry found there was suspicion of her involvement with some mysterious deaths and illnesses at her previous posting, Bexar County Hospital in San

Antonio. An official report stated that of the thirty-five children who expired during 1981, twenty-five had died on the three-to-eleven shift, which was Nurse Jones's shift. Around the hospital, that shift was being called the "Death Shift."

Kern County was slowly building a case against Genene Jones. District Attorney Ron Sutton was assigned to the case. At this point all of the statistics pointed to Genene's guilt. But all of the evidence was purely circumstantial. It was going to be hard to prove that Genene had injected succinylcholine into these innocent children. This drug was untraceable—in a living person it metabolizes quickly and breaks down into chemicals that naturally occur in the body. As a result, it has long been known as the drug of choice for doctors who want to commit murder.

But Ron Sutton had a trump card that he was hoping to play. He enlisted the help of a Swedish physician, Bo Holmstedt, who had developed a procedure to detect even minute quantities of succinylcholine in embalmed human tissue. An exhumation of Chelsea McCllelan was ordered. Dr. Fredric Rieders, who had worked with Dr. Holmstedt, gathered the tissue samples. The day of the exhumation was May 7, and on May 18, Ron Sutton got the phone call he was waiting for. Dr. Holmsted and Dr. Rieders confirmed that succinylcholine had been found in Chelsea's body.

Genene Jones went to trial for Chelsea's murder. Her lawyers tried to argue that Chelsea had died of natural causes. In Chelsea's first autopsy, it was discovered that she had scarring on her brain stem. Although not necessarily a lethal condition, defense pathologists theorized that this abnormality on Chelsea's brain stem may have led to her death.

The jury didn't buy it. They found Genene Jones guilty of murder, and sentenced her to ninety-nine years. Genene still had to face another trial for the illnesses and deaths thought to be caused by her in San Antonio. The children at Bexar County Hospital had developed seizures, bleeding, limpness, sudden urine output, breathing trouble, and irregular heartbeat. At least thirteen families were filing wrongful death suits against the hospital.

Exhumations were necessary to test for drugs in the children. Unfortunately, this hospital served many of the indigent in San Antonio, and many families were unable to have their children properly embalmed. As a result, the remains of some of the children could not be tested. The only charge that could be brought against Genene Jones was for injecting a baby with a blood-thinning drug called Heparin. The victim was a four-month-old male named Rolando Santos. Thanks to the intervention of the attending pediatrician, little Ronaldo cheated death.

Many of the administrators at Bexar County Hospital knew of the unexplained deaths. Nothing formally was done before Genene Jones left to continue her madness at Kerrville. There were numerous resignations and a shroud of secrecy. The victim's families filed lawsuits and most received out of court settlements.

Genene Jones tried to appeal her two convictions, but without success. Her prison sentences total one-hundred fifty-nine years.

An epidemiologist presented a interesting perspective on this case. During the trial, he presented some horrifying statistics to the jury. Pediatric ICU death rates in Genene Jones's unit soared 178 percent during 1980 and 1981. A fifteen month period that spanned from April 1981 through June 1982 had seen the early demise of forty-two children, 81 percent dying on the three-to-eleven shift. The study found that a child cared for by Genene Jones was ten times more likely to die than one being cared for by another nurse. All children were twenty-five times more likely to suffer a seizure during the three-to-eleven shift when Genene was working.

Genene is a perfect example of a rare syndrome known as

Munchausen Syndrome by Proxy. It firs appeared in medical literature in 1977, and was named for Baron von Munchausen, a nineteenth-century soldier famous for fabricating incredible tales of his battlefield exploits He spun these stories—in which he was invariably the hero—in order to draw attention to himself. Munchausen Syndrome refers to some people, mostly men, who compulsively make up, and then believe, these stories about themselves. The inability to tell the difference between fantasy and reality is the hallmark of the syndrome. When questioned about the "fantasy" story sufferers of the syndrome will maintain the story and continue believing the fantasy—even if facts come to light that prove it to be just that—a fantasy.

Interestingly, Munchausen Syndrome by Proxy usually involves women. Sufferers either lie about or actually create illnesses in their own children—or in Genene's case, children in her care—in order to get attention directed at themselves. Psychiatrists say it's rooted in feelings of abandonment, which creates a need for notoriety that ultimately cannot be satisfied.

A typical profile of a Munchausen Syndrome by Proxy sufferer is someone who is fascinated by the medical profession. In fact, more than a third of the people diagnosed with the syndrome are nurses. They will demand second and third opinions from doctors about illnesses in either themselves or their children, for which there are no actual symptoms. When doctors tell them there is nothing wrong they will develop a grudge against the profession as a whole, and are often openly contemptuous of health-care workers, especially if they're coworkers. They have a family history of siblings with similar problems, will often have an unexplained sibling death, and they often have trouble maintaining emotional relationships

Genene fit this profile in almost all of its particulars. She spent hours at the doctor getting assessed for illnesses that didn't exist; she often complained to coworkers that all the doctors they worked with were "layabouts" and "incompetents;" she had no enduring relationships, even with members of her family.

Genene, like Baron von Munchausen, wanted to be the hero. Sadly, she chose young children as the vehicle. Some experts believe she may not have actually wanted her victims to die. They feel she wanted them to come as close as possible to death, and then live, so that she could get credit for saving them. The problem for Genene, like a lot of people with this syndrome, is that the attention becomes addictive. They keep going and going until eventually they go too far and someone gets killed. You would think someone capable of thinking through a scheme like this would look like the picture of evil. Think again. If you check out the episode you'll see video and photos of Genene Jones. She looks like a sweet-hearted kindergarten teacher. Even some of her coworkers had trouble believing she was capable of such an elaborate ruse, but the facts were overwhelmingly against her.

To this day, Genene Jones maintains that children she killed and harmed were suffering from legitimate medical problems and she was only trying to save them. That's also a main feature of Munchausen Syndrome by Proxy. You could put Genene on a polygraph today, and if you asked whether she harmed those children she would say no and pass the polygraph with flying colors.

To produce this episode we needed a lot of children. For two days our production offices were filled with the young sons, daughters, nieces, nephews, and grandchildren of our staff. It was quite a party, although you'd never know it by watching the episode. There's no blood, knives, guns, or violence of the typical sort, yet it's one of the most harrowing stories we've ever done.

Some of these cases are so notorious that they become the subjects of books and movies. Genene's case is in a book entitled *The Death Shift*. This next story was the subject of a made-for-TV movie that starred Melissa Gilbert and Gregory Harrison. We called it "Dew Process" because, believe it or not, the weather played a key role in the killer's conviction.

Shortly after 7:00 on the morning of Saturday, August 30, 1986, police in Wilkes Barre, Pennsylvania, received an urgent call from a local resident named Neil Wolsieffer. He told them that minutes earlier he had been summoned across the street to the house of his brother, Dr. Glen Wolsieffer, who been attacked and was falling in and out of consciousness. Neil said he was unsure of the condition of his brother's wife, Betty, and their five-year-old daughter, Danielle.

When police arrived five minutes later Dr. Wolsieffer was fully conscious and appeared dazed. Neil told them that he had not left his brother's side—in other words, he had not gone upstairs to check on the other occupants of the house. Dr. Wolsieffer told police that an intruder had broken in and had attempted to strangle him; he was unsure if the intruder was still in the house.

Police went upstairs and saw that a bedroom Dr. Wolsieffer used as an office had been ransacked. In another bedroom, five-year-old Danielle was asleep unharmed. In the master bedroom police discovered the body of Betty Wolsieffer—it was on the floor, wrapped in a bundle of sheets. There were bruise marks around her neck, and rigor mortis had sent in. It appeared that Betty Wolsieffer had been strangled to death some hours earlier.

There were no foreign fingerprints in the home. Some blue fibers, apparently from jeans, were found, but no other trace evidence was present. Nothing was missing from the home, so robbery was eliminated as a motive. In fact, there was no apparent motive for anyone to have entered the home—except to kill Betty Wolsieffer, yet the investigation into her background found no one with a motive to kill her.

Dr. Wolsieffer was admitted to a local hospital. He had only minor injuries—some scratches on his chest and a long, linear bruise on the back of his neck. Dr. Wolsieffer's account of what had happened in his house was unclear; he claimed the blow he had received clouded his memory. He told police he thought the intruder had entered the house through an upstairs window—one that had a torn screen. He said that at one point the intruder had tried to strangle him from behind with some sort of string or rope, but that he had been able to work his hands through the front of the ligature. The intruder gave up, and struck Dr. Wolsieffer over the head. He said he didn't know what happened next. In fact, he wasn't even the one who discovered his wife's body.

Police had no witnesses, little evidence, and apparently no one with a motive to kill their victim.

Six weeks passed and the case looked like it might go cold. So police turned to Neil Wolsieffer—he was the first on the scene and might be of some help once his memory was jogged. But Neil he was reluctant to assist the investigation. He believed police had marked his brother as the prime suspect, and when he asked them point-blank they told Neil that his brother was the only suspect. They said they did not suspect Neil, but wanted to know if he had gone upstairs on the night of the murder. Neil clammed up. He said was unwilling to take a lie detector test, which caused a sensation in the local media.

Betty Wolsieffer's parents contacted Neil and pleaded with him to talk to investigators. He told them he could no longer take the pressure from newspapers, television and the community, and that he would meet with police. He called them to make an appointment and investigators were convinced they would finally get information that would break the case. The next day, on the way to that meeting, Neil Wolsieffer drove his car into an oncoming tractor trailer and was killed instantly. His death was ruled a suicide. His wife remembered him saying, as he was leaving the house, "I can't do anything to hurt my brother."

His death brought the investigation to a virtual halt. Ten months passed before police got another lead. A friend of Betty Wolsieffer's named Barbara Wende said that just a few day's before her death Betty said she had had it with her husband's infidelities and was finally going to tell him that if he couldn't stick to his marriage vows she was leaving and taking their daughter with her. It was widely known in the small town of Wilkes-Barre that Dr. Wolsieffer was carrying on two affairs, one with a hygienist in his office and the other with a former high school cheerleader.

It appeared Dr. Wolsieffer had a motive to kill his wife, but then a twenty-two-year-old woman by the name of Tracie Winter said she had committed the crime. But Winter was unstable and had attempted suicide on a number of occasions. Her story was ruled out when third parties accounted for her whereabouts on the night in question.

At this point all police had on Dr. Wolsieffer was circumstantial evidence; prosecutors were therefore wary about bringing charges. The case sat for more than two years, until a new District Attorney was elected and pledged to bring the case to a resolution. He enlisted two veteran state police officers to restart the investigation from the ground up.

Dr. John Coe, a forensic pathologist, told them it was a reasonable medical certainty that the wound on Dr. Wolsieffer's chest was self-inflicted. Even worse, an analysis of his neck injury contradicted his version of events. This injury was a thin, uninterrupted mark on the back of the neck from earlobe to earlobe. This did not gibe with Dr. Wolseiffer's story that he had been choked from behind and had worked his fingers up through the front of the ligature to prevent his strangulation. Dr. Coe also stated that distinct marks from Dr. Wolsieffer's own fingers would have been left on the front of his neck if his story were true. There were no such marks. In addition, there were no marks on Dr. Wolsieffer's hands, as there should have been if they'd been caught up in the ligature.

The bruises on Betty's face and her split lip indicated that there may have been a fight.

Prosecutors brought in famed FBI profiler John Douglas, who said the crime was most likely committed by someone who knew Betty Wolsieffer well. He thought the ransacked office was a ploy designed to throw investigators. He said Dr. Wolsieffer's injuries were not consistent with loss of consciousness and that he had ample time to alter the crime scene after Betty's death. Like the investigators, he concluded that Dr. Wolsieffer was the likely killer.

Prosecutors thought this could have accounted for the mark on the back of Dr. Wolsieffer's neck. They thought it was possible that the mark came from Betty yanking, and breaking, a gold chain Dr. Wolsieffer usually wore around his neck. This would also account for scratch marks on Dr. Wolsieffer's chest.

Douglas Deedrick, and FBI hair and fiber expert, said the blue cotton fibers and blue denim fibers found under Betty's fingernails were consistent with jeans Dr. Wolsieffer wore on the night of the murder. Deedrick also checked the dye in the fibers. He admitted that an intruder could have been wearing similar jeans, but they would have had to be the exact type of jeans with the exact same indigo dye.

Police told of a phone call they had received from Dr. Wolsieffer days before the murder. He said that a window screen had been cut, possibly by a burglar. The night of Betty's murder the alleged point of entry was a second floor window—the same one that Dr. Wolsieffer spoke to police about. The intruder, according to Dr. Wolsieffer's story, cut the screen after gain-

Glen and Betty Wolsieffer in happier times. His philandering led to her murder.

ing access to the roof with a ladder in the rear of the home, and may have done so in the days before the murder.

The ladder, however, was cracked and was left standing backward against the rear of the house. Dr. Wolsieffer had used this ladder in the past, when he returned home from late night trysts with his girlfriends. If there had been an intruder, there was no sign of him on the ladder; there was also no sign of indentation on the ground below the window, which indicated that no one had been on the ladder the night of the murder.

Finally, Dr. Joseph Sobel, a forensic meteorologist, provided some unusual, and ultimately damning testimony against Dr. Wolsieffer. Sobel analyzed the water vapor conditions on the night of the murder. He said it was unlikely that an intruder walking on the roof the of Wolsieffer home—Dr. Wolsieffer's story was that the intruder had come in through an upstairs bedroom—would leave no footprints. Temperature and humidity records for the night in question indicated that so much dew would have been on the roof that some footprints should have been visible. Sobel also stated that Dr. Wolsieffer's car would have been covered with dew if, as Dr. Wolsieffer claimed, it had not been driven since he returned home at about 2.30 A.M. The car was bone dry.

Prosecutors, piecing together the evidence and Dr. Wolsieffer's actions before and immediately after the murder, came up with a theory about what happened. They said that Dr. Wolsieffer had met his mistress for a sexual encounter at a local hotel on the afternoon before the murder. A few hours later he met his other mistress at a nightclub. He was seen leaving about 2.30 A.M. When he got home his wife probably confronted him about his infidelities; she told a friend she was going to do so and his coming home so late probably sparked the fatal fight.

Police believe he attacked Betty on the bed, and that it was his fingers that had made the marks on her neck. While trying to defend herself she scratched his chest, and then grabbed the gold necklace he always wore around his neck. She pulled down on it so hard it eventually broke, but not before causing the long, linear bruise on the back of the doctor's neck. Now that she was dead he was seized with remorse, and psychologist said this may account for his cleaning the body and changing the nightgown. Still, he had to get rid of the gown, and police believe he got in his car and threw them in a river about a quarter mile from the house, which is why there was no dew on his car.

He then tried to stage the crime scene by placing the ladder—backward—at the back of the house, and then going inside the house to slash the window screen and make it appear to be the killer's point of entry. To make it seem as if the intruder attacked him Dr. Wolsieffer had to injure himself. Police are

Still from police video. The ladder allegedly used by the killer. Forensic analysis revealed it was only a prop.

still unsure how he did this, but believe he may have thrown himself down a flight of stairs.

Dr. Wolsieffer then called his brother, Neil, and here is one of the strangest parts of the story. Neil never went upstairs to check on Betty or the Wolsieffer's young daughter. Police theorize that Dr. Wolsieffer may have told his brother what really happened—that Betty was already dead and that he'd killer her. It appears that out to his brother Neil agreed to help cover up the crime. Eventually, however, the burden was too great, and torn between his brother and the truth, Neil killed himself.

Dr. Wolsieffer's intruder story did not impress the jurors in his case. But they did rule that his actions were not premeditated. Almost six years after his wife's murder he was convicted of third degree murder and sentenced to eight to twenty years in prison.

Twelve years into his sentence Dr. Wolsieffer, by all accounts a model prisoner, was offered the opportunity of parole. Prosecutors told him he could walk out a free man if he would only admit in court that he had killed his wife. He flatly refused and is expected to serve the full 20 year sentence.

With this case, as in so many others, we had to go "back to school." So many different sciences play into the prosecution of crimes that we often find ourselves poring over textbooks or talking to experts about things we learned (or were supposed to learn) years ago. It's almost as if we are studying for a test. Meteorology was the discipline of the day in the Wolsieffer case, and we were lucky to have the services of Dr. Joe Sobel, who, in addition to being a forensic meteorologist, is also a top executive at Accu-Weather, one of the leading providers of weather information to television and radio stations across the country. "Dr. Joe," as he's called, gave us a useful primer in the role weather played in the conviction of Dr. Wolsieffer. And here it is:

Dew does not fall. It's created by air temperature combining with moisture present in the air; the higher the temperature of the air the more moisture—water vapor, actually—that it can hold. Obviously, if you cool the temperature of air it will be able to hold less moisture. That's why you don't see dew in the middle of a summer afternoon; you see it in the morning, after the temperature has dropped. The moment at which the water vapor turns from gas to water is called the saturation point or the dew point. It happens more quickly on things like the metal surface of a car because that cools faster than something like dirt, or cement.

Betty Wolsieffer was murdered in the dog days of August. In fact, the day before her death was hot and clear. Dr. Sobel checked weather conditions for that night and found there was no rain, a light wind, and surprisingly cool temperatures. In short, this was a night where there would have been a lot of moisture in the air, and because of the large drop in temperature, a lot of dew would have been formed. When Dr. Wolsieffer's car was analyzed the morning of the murder it was dry. If, as he claimed, it hadn't been driven for at least four hours it would have had dew on it. In fact, his wife's car, which in a police videotape, can be seen right next to his, is soaking wet.

A running joke among the team that shoots our re-creations is "you have to sacrifice for your art." This is usually directed at actors who are not as accustomed to our crew to standing around in all varieties of weather—blistering heat, sub-zero wind chills, and all the rest, waiting for their scene to begin. In this case the "sacrifice" had to do with simulating the fatal fight between Dr. Wolsieffer and his wife. In real life it was obviously violent, and we wanted to re-create this violence but did not want to hurt our actors in the process.

The two actors said they were willing to try anything. So we explained to them exactly what police believed transpired on the Wolsieffer's bed, which meant they would have to tumble off the bed and onto the floor while going at each other the entire time. If you see the scene, you'll see what we mean by "sacrificing for their art." The two actors, who'd only met each other a couple of hours earlier, fought as if their lives depended on it. They actually flew off the bed with such force that a lamp inadvertently got knocked off a nightstand and landed on top of them. The producers thought it looked great on the monitors but rushed onto the set when the take was finished because they were convinced someone had to have suffered a serious injury.

Instead they found the actors brushing themselves off and prepared for further "sacrifices." Luckily, for them and for us, the single take was plenty real enough.

While Glen Wolsieffer may not have planned his wife's murder, there's no question that the doctor in a case we called "Bitter Pill" had plenty of time to think his plan through. How do we know? Because he was caught on surveillance videotape—twice.

Michelle Baker was a paramedic who had given up on love, until a friend who worked for a local doctor introduced her to a soft-spoken, charming medical resident, Dr. Maynard Muntzing. Dr. Muntzing was the same age as Michelle, they shared many interests and a strong sexual attraction. Their whirlwind love affair could have come from the pages of a romance novel. Within weeks of meeting they were engaged to be married.

Dr. Muntzing moved into Michelle's small home in Huber Heights, Ohio, and soon she became pregnant. Dr. Muntzing said he was ecstatic, and to celebrate the pregnancy, they took a trip to Florida. On their first night there Dr. Muntzing asked Michelle if they could postpone the wedding so all of his family could be there. Michelle was disappointed, but agreed. That night at dinner Dr. Muntzing brought her a virgin pina colada—she didn't want to drink alcohol because of her pregnancy—that tasted unusually bitter. She drank it and thought nothing more of it.

Later that night Michelle experienced severe cramps and some light bleeding; Dr. Muntzing assured her she was fine. Michelle later visited her family doctor in Ohio and he also told her there was nothing to worry about. She looked forward to having a baby and getting married.

And there was every reason to be happy. Dr. Muntzing purchased a three-hundred twenty-thousand dollar home in which they would raise their new child, and repeatedly expressed happiness about his impending fatherhood.

But Michelle's pregnancy was proving to be difficult. The severe cramps and bleeding were becoming more regular and she became concerned about the baby. Dr. Muntzing assured her that everything would be alright and that the problems were a normal part of pregnancy. He said her concerns were nothing more than the jitters experienced by most first-time mothers to be.

Soon, however, Michelle got some devastating news that had nothing to do with the baby. Dr. Muntzing told her he was still involved with his former girlfriend, Tammy Erwin, and that he was going to marry her. Heartbroken, Michelle spent the Fourth of July holiday alone. Dr. Muntzing said he was going fishing with a friend in Columbus, an hour's drive away.

That night, Michelle heard a familiar voice while listening to the request-line segment of a local radio show; the caller identified himself as "Maynard," and requested a song for his girlfriend, "Tammy." Michelle soon concluded that Dr. Muntzing lied to her and was across town with his girlfriend. She drove to Tammy's house and confronted Dr. Muntzing. After a heated altercation, Michelle said the relationship was over and told Dr. Muntzing to move out.

A few days later, he called to apologize and invited Michelle on a picnic so they could talk and perhaps reconcile. But shortly after they sat down—shortly after she drank some cola he brought with him—Michelle became sick. She went to her doctor, who performed an ultrasound and determined, to her relief, that the baby was still perfectly healthy.

Michelle's relationship with Dr. Muntzing continued to improve, but her health was taking a turn for the worse. The cramping and bleeding continued, and she had horrible spells of nausea and vomiting. Michelle's twin sister, Malinda, had what at first seemed to be an outlandish theory about Michelle's illness. Since Michelle only became sick when she was with Dr. Muntzing, Malinda suspected he might have something to do with it. Michelle recalled that Dr. Muntzing was the one who brought drinks to their table at the restaurant in Florida–shortly before she first became ill. He also prepared her drink at their picnic, and she became sick soon afterward.

Michelle had to admit that as unlikely as it seemed, it was possible her doctor/boyfriend might be trying to harm her. The more she thought about it the less she trusted him. So when Dr. Muntzing told Michelle he was taking his two children from a previous marriage to Disney World, she didn't believe it. She drove to Tammy Erwin's house and through an open window, she heard Dr. Muntzing and Tammy discussing her pregnancy. Dr. Muntzing told Tammy the pregnancy would be "taken care of," and suddenly Michelle suspected her sister was right—that the doctor might be trying to kill her baby.

Her suspicions were intensified when Dr. Muntzing told her the relationship was over. He informed Michelle that he had married Tammy, his former girlfriend. He said he still wanted to remain friends because, after all, Michelle was going to be the mother of his baby. Michelle was devastated, and now had to admit, however reluctantly, that Dr. Muntzing had clear motive to harm the baby. His new wife was not likely to react favorably to her husband being the father of a child who was not hers—especially with the birth falling within months of their marriage.

Michelle went to local police with her suspicions and they were skeptical. Michelle seemed to be the odd person out in a love triangle and it wouldn't be the first time they'd seen someone go to outlandish extremes to get revenge. Detectives wanted Michelle to take a lie detector test, but departmental rules prohibited administering the test to pregnant women. Michelle decided she had to take matters into her own hands.

She enlisted her neighbor and they devised a plan. They hid a small video camera in Michelle's kitchen, and the next time Dr. Muntzing came to Michelle's house for dinner, they made sure he was alone in the kitchen to get some drinks. The camera recorded some chilling images. Dr. Muntzing pulled a vial

Still from police surveillance video. This picture tells the whole story.

from his pocket. It was filled with some kind of liquid. He looked around to make sure he wasn't being watched and dumped the contents into Michelle's drink.

This time she was ready. She had a plastic container and another drink hidden in the bathroom. She went in, dumped the contents of the drink Dr. Muntzing had made her into the container, and emerged with the decoy drink in hand. He watched her as she drank it. She wondered: could it be possible that the man she once loved was really capable of trying to harm her and their baby?

To find out Michelle took the drink he'd made her and brought it to local detectives. It was clear—even to the naked eye—that something had been done to the drink. A thick sludge had settled to the bottom, and investigators theorized that it might be the abortion pill, RU-486, or perhaps a cancer drug. Samples of the drink were placed in a gas chromatograph/mass spectrometer, and it was found to contain large amounts of Cytotec, a drug used to treat stomach ulcers. All containers of Cytotec carry a clear warning stating it should never be used by pregnant women since it will induce abortion.

But police had a problem. They couldn't prove that Dr. Muntzing had drugged Michelle's drink. They had her surveillance videotape, which was convincing but shaky evidence. Since the tape had been made by the complainant in the case it might get thrown out of court. So police decided to make a tape of their own. In Michelle's kitchen, inside a ceramic figurine of a firefighter saving a baby, they concealed a tiny video camera. Michelle called Dr. Muntzing and invited him to dinner. She said that even though their romance was over they would soon be parents of a newborn baby and needed to reconcile their differences.

While two police officers hid in Michelle's garage with a television monitor, Dr. Muntzing arrived. The conversation was casual, even friendly. Michelle left the kitchen to put steaks on the grill and, as if on cue, Dr. Muntzing went to the kitchen to prepare drinks. As police watched, he washed his hands, pulled a vial from his pocket, and dumped the contents into one of the glasses.

Police arrested him on the spot. Dr. Muntzing told them he was only putting a prenatal vitamin in the drink. When they told him they suspected that lab tests would confirm it was Cytotec, he realized that they knew what he'd been doing to Michelle. Police checked the doctor's Jaguar and found a full bottle of Cytotec in the glove compartment.

Dr. Muntzing was arrested on a charge of attempted murder.

Shortly before the trial, twenty-eight weeks into her pregnancy, Michelle delivered a stillborn baby. The cause of the baby's death was marked "undetermined," because the coroner found no trace of Cytotec in the placenta. The reason? When Michelle began to suspect that her boyfriend/doctor was feeding her poison she refused to drink anything he gave her. As a result, all traces of Cytotec had left the baby's system, even though enough had been ingested to cause its death.

Michelle would have to testify against Dr. Muntzing and prosecutors were worried that the strain of losing her baby combined with a trial would simply be too much for her, so they made a deal.

Dr. Muntzing's wife, Tammy, pleaded guilty to a charge of filling the prescription for Cytotec and was placed on probation. Dr. Muntzing pleaded guilty to contaminating a substance for human consumption and attempted felonious assault. He was sentenced to five years in prison, was forced to give up his Ohio medical license and the right to apply for a medical license in any other state.

If you read this and feel that Dr. Muntzing cheated justice you wouldn't be alone. Michelle felt the same way, and so, apparently did the judge. At Michelle's request, Dr. Muntzing was forced to watch a videotape of the baby's stillborn birth. Michelle, who named the baby Makayla, still keeps the ashes in her house.

As for the doctor, he had to stipulate in court that he actually did try to kill Michelle's unborn child. Strangely, or, given the circumstances, perhaps not so strangely, he doesn't seem able to fully come to grips with what he's done. In front of a crowded courtroom he makes a rambling speech in which he says something about "knocking the dust from his sandals," and "moving on." The odd thing to consider—among many odd things in the case—is that he had two young children of his own.

This episode shows the video that Michelle shot with a hidden camera. By a stroke of luck she got a perfect angle. It was impossible to predict exactly where the doctor would try to spike the drink but she took her best guess and he walks right to his "mark," almost as if he were an actor following direction. It's rare to catch a killer in the act on-camera, but it's all there in the show, and it's pretty disturbing, especially when you consider he's trying to kill his own child.

As of this writing Dr. Muntzing is still in jail, and prosecutors say they're determined to keep tabs on him after he gets out to make absolutely sure he never practices medicine again.

SEVEN

The Crime of the Twentieth Century

The assassination of President John F. Kennedy is quite possibly one of the most fascinating forensic cases of the twentieth century. The television coverage in 1963, crude by today's standards, was compelling nevertheless and held a nation in its thrall. On live television, we watched as the prime suspect, Lee Harvey Oswald, was led through police headquarters on his way to a more secure location. It would be the last we'd see him. A man jumped from the shadows, pointed a handgun at Oswald's stomach, then shot and killed him. The killer, Jack Ruby, was a Dallas strip-club owner with alleged ties to organized crime.

Forty years after the event, hours of television time on the major networks and cable were devoted to reexamining that shocking day in Dallas and the conspiracy theories that have followed in its wake. *Forensic Files* took part in the general reexamination, applying its own special insights into those deadly moments that changed world history.

In 1963, the murder of a president was not even a federal crime. The last president who had died in office was Franklin Roosevelt nearly twenty years earlier; the last president who had been assassinated was William McKinley in 1901. Naturally, a certain confusion was part of the investigation. Who was responsible for doing what? How would they proceed?

A week after the shooting, President Lyndon Johnson assembled the U.S. Commission to Report upon the Assassination of President John F. Kennedy to investigate the crime. It was to have no restrictions in its powers and quickly became known as the Warren Commission because it was headed by Chief Justice Earl Warren.

About a year after the assassination, The Warren Commission released its findings in a twenty-six volume report. The Report concluded that Lee Harvey Oswald, acting alone, killed President Kennedy and wounded Governor John Connally as they rode in a motorcade through Dallas Texas.

The report was criticized almost immediately. First, by most accounts, President Kennedy's autopsy was poorly handled. It was performed by pathologists who primarily worked in a hospital and were more accustomed to finding cancer cells in a tissue sample than they were at analyzing gunshot wounds. Reportedly, the two lead pathologists handling the president's autopsy had never seen a gunshot wound before.

Oswald's background was suspicious. He had been in the U.S. Marines, then had defected to the Soviet Union, moved back to the United States, was a sympathizer of the Castro regime, allegedly had ties with members of U.S. Intelligence, and then was himself murdered while in police custody by a man who had links to the Mafia. Could this all be a coincidence?

Finally, the Warren Report concluded three shots were fired from the Texas School Book Depository behind the presidential motorcade, where Oswald was employed. One shot missed.

Another struck both President Kennedy and Texas Governor John Connally sitting in front of the president, and the third was the president's fatal head wound.

A Dallas businessman, Abraham Zapruder, captured the assassination on his 8-millimeter movie camera. It is, without question, the most famous home movie in history. The Zapruder film clearly shows President Kennedy's head moving backward at the fatal impact, not forward as one would expect.

And skeptics had difficulty believing that one bullet could have entered President Kennedy's back, exited his throat, then hit Governor Connally in the right armpit, shattering a rib, then exited under his right nipple, shattering his right wrist before entering his thigh. This bullet was discovered in almost pristine condition on a stretcher in Parkland Hospital. Dr. Cyril Wecht questioned this single-bullet hypothesis and dubbed it "the magic bullet."

Complicating matters for the Warren Commission were witnesses who said they heard more than three shots. Others said they heard shots coming from in front of the president, from the so-called grassy knoll. One witness claimed to have seen a puff of smoke from this same area.

By the 1980s, polls indicated that as many as 80 percent of Americans did not believe Oswald acted alone. The very fact that the Warren Commission was composed of such eminent leaders stimulated the belief that there was a cover-up at the highest levels. Other independent investigations concluded the opposite, that there were two or more shooters in Dealy Plaza that day. When Gerald Posner published his lengthy best-seller *Case Closed: Lee Harvey Oswald and the Assassination of JFK* in 1993, he carefully refuted each of the conspiracy theories. For all his meticulous evidence, the case remained distinctly open in many of the people's minds.

In 2001, a new study appeared in a respected British forensic journal that determined, among other things, that there

were four shots fired. As the fortieth anniversary of the assassination approached, we suggested doing a detailed forensic
analysis of the assassination in a *Forensic Files* special. The executives at Court TV enthusiastically agreed. We would let the
viewers decide for themselves whether Oswald committed the
crime, or whether there were more shooters and therefore, a
wider conspiracy.

Forensic science was quite advanced in 1963, but not nearly
as sophisticated as it is today. What new techniques that were
not available before then might be applied to the old evidence?
What might we learn?

The special took more than one year to produce and was one
of the most complex and complicated projects we've ever encountered.

We began by reading the Warren report. It's dry, detailed,
poorly organized and utterly fascinating. Most surprising was
the wealth of forensic evidence in the case that seldom makes
its way into the media.

Handwriting analysis of a money order showed that Lee Harvey Oswald bought the rifle found on the sixth floor of the
Texas School Book Depository. When arrested, fibers from the
shirt Oswald was wearing were microscopically similar to fibers
found on the rifle. Oswald's palm print was found on the gun,
in a location visible when the gun was disassembled. Ballistic
evidence linked bullet fragments found in the limousine to
Oswald's rifle.

Here's another thing we found interesting: The entry wound
on Governor Connally's back was oblong, not round. This indicated that the bullet was tumbling when it hit him. Bullets
tumble after they hit something first.

It was obvious from the start that we'd need forensic animation to visualize the shooting. In 1991, an engineering firm,
Failure Analysis Associates (now called Exponent Inc.) went to

Dealy Plaza with a digital surveying system to map the crime scene to within a hundredth of an inch. They also measured the presidential limousine, built a plywood replica, placed two men inside who approximated President Kennedy and Governor Connally in size and weight then positioned them in the limousine in the positions shown in the Zapruder film. Then, they captured the images digitally.

As the engineers were digitizing the Zapruder film frame-by-frame, Jeff Lotz of Failure Associates noticed something that had up to that point been unnoticed. At frame number 224, Connally's lapel flips up from his chest. A film frame passes so rapidly that the human eye can't see it: sixty-thousandths of a second, according to Dr. Roger McCarthy of Failure Associates, twice as fast as a human eye is capable of capturing an image. Since the bullet that exited Connally did so under his right nipple in the vicinity of his right lapel flap, Failure Analysis experts concluded this was the bullet going through him.

Failure Analysis produced their own forensic animation of the assassination back in 1991. It was very well done for its time, but used fifteen-year-old software. To show viewers something more contemporary, we took that animation, the Dealey Plaza survey measurements, the Zapruder film and headed to New Hampshire, the home of Hatchling Studios, one of the finest 3-D animation firms we could find.

When we got there, the office walls were covered with every photograph of the assassination they could find. They had divided their team of animators into specialties: One group worked only on the bullet, another group worked in the rifle, others concentrated on the limousine, the placement of the men inside the car, and so on. They spent hundreds of hours on minute details that would fly past a viewer in seconds.

After creating the Dealey Plaza computer model, the chief animator, Marc Dole, placed the limousine into position at the moment the bullet passed through both the president and gov-

A re-creation of Oswald walking into the Texas School Book Depository with a paper package he said were curtain rods. Forensic analysis found evidence the rifle was inside.

A look-alike actor portraying Oswald in the sixth floor window of the Texas School Book Depository. This scene was cut from the domestic version of the show but left in for the international version.

The re-creation of Abraham Zapruder filming the JFK assassination, the most famous home movie in history. Zapruder was standing on a pedestal and was afraid of heights. His secretary was holding him so he wouldn't fall.

ernor. He then placed the two animated figures inside the car, with the governor's position as shown in the Zapruder film. Since President Kennedy was behind the street sign at this moment, we approximated his position using the first frame of film when he was in view.

Many drawings and re-creations of the positions of the president and governor that you see in the conspiracy books are inaccurate. The one we see most often, the one shown in the movie *JFK*, shows the president and governor sitting on the same level, one in front of the other. But that's not they way they were sitting in the limousine.

President Kennedy was sitting higher in the back seat than the Governor Connally, who was sitting below and to the left of the president in the jump seat. The car was also pitched slightly downward, since it was heading toward the underpass.

3-D animation showing how the bullet passed through both President Kennedy and Governor Connally. Connally was seated lower than the president and slightly to his left, on a jump seat.

With these coordinates put into the animation, I asked Mark to draw a straight line from under Governor Connally's right nipple (the exit wound of the bullet) to the sixth-floor window of the School Book Depository just to see what it looked like. I then asked Mark to rotate the camera position so that I could see the limousine and School Book Depository from the front of the limousine. To my surprise, the wounds of Governor Connally and the president were in a straight line back to the sixth-floor window of the depository, the alleged snipers nest.

There's been a lot made of the fact that the wound in the president's back was going from low to high, not high to low as you would expect. An exhibit from the House Select Committee on Assassination in 1978 shows why.

Let us assume the president was hunched slightly forward at the moment he was hit in the upper back. (He was behind the highway sign at the time, so the Zapruder film cannot give this

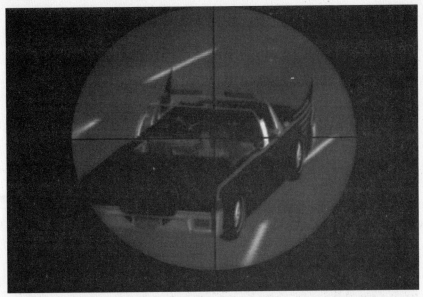

For one of the first times on television, viewers saw what the size, scale, and position of the people in the presidential limousine looked like through the scope of Oswald's rifle.

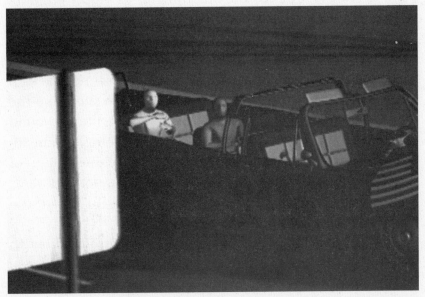

Animation matching the Zapruder film when the president is visible after passing the highway sign, moments after he was hit.

position accurately.) A bullet from the School Book Depository would pass through the president's back and through his throat as the bullet is heading downward. When the president was examined during the autopsy, with his back straight, the wound on the president's back was lower than his throat. fueling controversy that he was shot from street level, or even lower. It's an interesting example of how a wound's trajectory looks one way when the victim is flat on an autopsy table, but looks much different if you position the victim in the way he was when shot.

The animation also showed something we never quite realized. Conspiracy theorists point to the backward movement of the president's head as proof that the shot came from in front of the limousine rather than behind it. There had also been witnesses who said they heard shots fired in front of the president, from the so-called grassy knoll.

To test this hypothesis, once we created the model of Dealy Plaza to scale and placed the limousine in its proper position, we were able to look at the scene by placing the camera opposite Abraham Zapruder's position, on the other side of the limousine. We were surprised to see that President Kennedy's head was parallel to the grassy knoll area at the moment of the fatal head wound. Therefore, had the president been shot from the grassy knoll, as critics suggest, there would have been a wound in the side of the president's head, which there was not. In addition, if the president's head moved away from the location of the shot, his head would have moved sideways, not backward.

Why does the president's head move backward toward the bullet at impact?

Dr. John Lattimer, the first private physician permitted to examine the autopsy evidence, conducted a number of ballistic experiments showing that it was possible for a skull to move backward, toward the position of the rifle, at impact. This was due to the propulsion effect of the brain tissue which exited

Robert Berkovitz performing digital audio testing of the Dallas police tape many believe contains the gunfire of assassins.

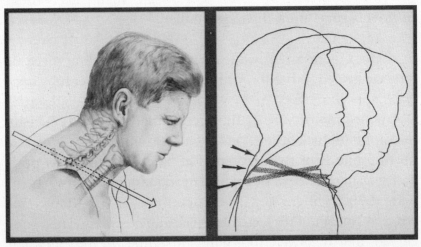

A drawing of the president when the bullet passed through his throat heading toward Governor Connally. If you analyze the angle of trajectory when the president is lying flat on an autopsy table, it appears the shot came from behind the president at a low angle . . . but not when taking into account his position in the limousine at the time.

from the front. He used human skulls filled with animal tissue for these tests.

Noted forensic pathologist Dr. Michael Baden correctly points out that Dr. Lattimer's experiments shouldn't be construed as scientific proof of this phenomenon, since Dr. Lattimer's tests weren't conducted at the proper trajectory or distance. Nevertheless, we included film of Dr. Lattimer's tests and let the viewers decide for themselves.

Finally, if a second shooter was involved, fragments from other bullets would have been found in the limousine and in the victims. Neutron activation analysis of bullet fragments taken from President Kennedy's head wound, and all of the fragments found in the limousine revealed it was highly likely they all came from the same bullet. In addition, a bullet fragment from Governor Connally's wrist was compared to a sample taken from the so-called magic bullet which the Warren Commission says went through both President Kennedy and Governor Connally. The result? Once again, highly likely these fragments came from the magic bullet.

In doing our research, we learned about a startling piece of forensic evidence that the Warren commission never fully analyzed.

A police motorcycle in the presidential motorcade had its microphone stuck in the "on" position. Some believe it picked up the sounds of the assassination, and were recorded on a police Dictaphone back at police headquarters.

In 1978 a congressional subcommittee had the tape analyzed by a team of respected forensic audio experts. They concluded that there were four gunshot sounds on the tape, one more than Lee Harvey Oswald could have fired. They also concluded that one of those four shots originated in front of the president, from the so-called grassy knoll.

In the years since, various forensic experts have disputed

these findings. So Court TV and *Forensic Files* commissioned a new analysis by Robert Berkovitz, the retired chairman of Sensimetrics an audio research firm headquartered in Boston, Massachusetts.

Berkovitz began his six-month investigation by carefully reviewing the methods and conclusions of all the earlier researchers. Then, he analyzed the tape.

First, Berkovitz found no evidence of motorcycle engine sounds as one would expect if the recording was made by a microphone on a police motorcycle driving down the street, going around corners.

Second, the sounds on the tape, previously identified as gunshots (and echoes) were similar in all respects to other sound peaks on the tape that had not been identified as gunfire or echoes.

And when a computer generated random noise, those sound waves appeared strikingly similar to the soundwaves on this tape.

As Berkovitz told *Forensic Files*, "We're unable to find any evidence that in fact there's a gunshot on the recording."

Berkovitz's findings support the view held by retired Dallas Sheriff Bowles, who was the police dispatcher on the day of the assassination. Bowles discovered there was a second police motorcycle with a faulty microphone switch that day in Dallas. It was parked near the Dallas Trade Mart where President Kennedy was headed for a luncheon speech. Bowles is convinced that this motorcycle, parked next to a Dallas Police cruiser, was the unit recording the sounds captured on the police dispatchers tape.

Also, on the tape at the time of the alleged gunshots, Berkovitz heard the voice of the Dallas sheriff, saying "Hold everything secure until homicide investigators get there." The sheriff made this statement about a minute after the assassination. Berkovitz's tests found that this was recorded onto the tape *when it was transmitted* and wasn't the result of cross-talk or a recording error made while copying the tapes. Bowles says this happened, because this announcement came over the speaker of the police cruiser and was picked up by the microphone on the motorcycle parked next to it.

If there was an elusive grassy-knoll shooter, he left not one shred of scientific evidence behind. After forty years of investigation by scientists, researchers, journalists and conspiracy buffs, no one has come up with any scientific evidence of anyone shooting from anywhere other than the School Book Depository.

In his book, *Case Closed*, Gerald Posner wrote, "For those seeking the truth, the facts are incontrovertible. Chasing shadows on the grassy knoll will never substitute for real history. Lee Harvey Oswald, driven by his own twisted and impenetrable furies, was the only assassin at Dealey Plaza on November 22, 1963."

We think he's right.

EIGHT
Too Hot for Air

S ometimes we come up with cases that, for one reason or another, are just too hot for the networks to handle. David Letterman is famous for his unflattering stories about network executives in his monologues. Audiences enjoy hearing some of the wacky, ridiculous things network executives say when trying to settle the various disputes and issues that arise during the production of a network television show.

Creative people and network executives often disagree; it's the nature of their roles.

As a group, network executives are fun, funny, smart, sophisticated, well-versed in pop culture and great sources for gossip. You'll never meet a nicer group of people. Most of the problems producers and other creative people have with network executives occur because, for whatever reason, many network executives have never produced a television program. It's like a coach of a pro sports team who never played the game professionally. Players will inevitably question their judgment if they perceive the coach doesn't understand the game from the player's perspective.

None of this is to say that disagreements between producers and the network get nasty. Far from it. You don't get to be a network producer without mastering the art of respectful disagreement. Those who haven't usually don't last long.

"True crime" programming poses problems that other genres don't. Crime scene pictures, interviews about autopsy findings, and crime re-creations are often good for ratings but frighten advertisers.

Networks are careful about what they allow on the air, especially since the famous Janet Jackson Super Bowl incident. What astounds me is what the network rejects. You'd think that after approving an episode—the show's pilot—about a man who puts his wife through a woodchipper, that they would approve anything. Not so.

Nothing, not even a woodchipper is as frightening as the dreaded "b" word (as in bondage.)

Even people at the Playboy Channel cringe when they hear it, probably because it conjures up negative images of sado-masochism, although consensual bondage between partners isn't always like that.

One of my favorite writers, Ellen Harris, wrote a book entitled *Dying to Get Married*, about an affluent young woman, a newlywed, who was found dead inside her home after a house fire. The victim's husband was out of town on a business trip on the night of the fire. You see this one coming, don't you?

As I read Harris's book, I was completely hooked because of the intricacy of the case. The doors and windows of the home were all locked, with no signs of forced entry. The victim was found in the garage, tied to a chair. The bondage was intricate, time-consuming to do, the kind often used in consensual encounters. There was an empty champagne bottle lying by her side.

When police notified the victim's husband of her death, he appeared distraught. But he said he wasn't at all surprised by her murder. He claimed his wife asked him to include bondage in their love life, but he had always refused. He suspected his wife had engaged in that activity behind his back when he was away, although he had no idea why a lover would kill her.

The problem was, all of the victim's previous lovers said just the opposite. That she was conservative, shy, the type of woman ". . . who would make a missionary proud." Nothing in her background suggested any interest in alternative sexual lifestyles.

Inside the burned-out home, were remnants of a "to do" list in the husband's handwriting. At the top of the list was a reminder asking his wife to add him as the beneficiary of her life insurance policies. It was higher on the list than booking their honeymoon trip, which had been on hold since their wedding. Police also discovered the husband still maintained his old apartment and hadn't told his closest friends about his marriage.

I didn't even get to the forensic investigation before Court TV said "absolutely not." Their position was, murder is one thing, but bondage is another matter. They didn't want to listen to the outcry from the sales department trying to sell advertising in an episode like this, although, in my view, it's not much different than most of the other cases we do.

It's too bad, too, because the forensic science in this case was absolutely fascinating. The husband was eventually convicted, but not without much controversy. One fire expert says there are more convictions of innocent people in arson cases than in almost anything else. Why? Experts say its because most fires are investigated by arson investigators, who have a bias walking into to the scene, as opposed to fire investigators who are looking for the source of the fire, not proof that it was arson.

The network did approve another arson case which will

make an interesting show. It's about an elderly couple killed in a fire of their old home. Investigators were convinced that an flammable liquid was used because of the extreme heat of the fire and how quickly it spread. Tests did uncover remnants of an accelerant.

The couple probably should have been in a nursing home, since they needed so much daily care. They had only one son, who was the primary caregiver. He made comments to a friend, that the responsibility of his parents care was, at times, over-whelming.

Investigators charged him with their murder. The motive? Money, they say he killed them so he could get their money before it was spent on long term care. But, many years earlier, the couple's wood floors were refinished with an expensive coating, one that tests showed, was flammable. It was the kind used before new laws prohibiting flammable materials.

You see? Fire investigators are interesting. You'll have to watch to see how this episode turns out.

Networks are also sensitive about stories involving children. I proposed doing the case of a woman who walked into a hospital Emergency Room holding her newborn baby. She said she went into labor while running errands, stopped her car along the side of the road, handled the birth herself, unassisted, then drove to the nearest hospital.

The scientific angle began with the doctor in the emergency room who could tell just by looking at the baby's head that this was not a vaginal birth. The head was too round for that, and looked more like those he saw after a cesarian.

The blood on the woman's clothing appeared to have come from an angle different than what she was saying.

The hospital notified police, who found a car abandoned on a deserted stretch of road outside of town. The car belonged to a woman who was nine months pregnant. Nearby, in a shallow grave, was the missing woman. Her baby had been surgically removed with expert precision. The killer would have had only fifteen minutes or less, to remove the baby before dying from a lack of oxygen. On the umbilical cord was a bite mark.

Apparently, the killer faked her own pregnancy for months by wearing prosthetic devices like the ones actresses use in movies. Every month, she would wear a slightly larger size.

After the ninth month of the charade, the killer waited outside a local health club. This assured her the mother was taking good care of herself and the baby. She chose a victim, followed her, was somehow able to stop the victim along a deserted stretch of road, and you know the rest.

What I found fascinating was the perpetrator's husband. He insisted he knew nothing about the deception!

Court TV wanted no part of this one. They felt it was too raw, too horrifying a crime for prime-time television. My view was tempered by a desire to interview the husband. Can you imagine what kind of intimate life he shared with his wife not to notice that prosthesis? Yeah, don't say it. I'm wondering the same thing.

After the rejection, the programming executive who made the decision would try occasionally to sooth the ruffled feathers, but stopped when he noticed the steam coming from my ears!

In the summer of 2002, *Forensic Files* made television history. It was the first prime time television series from a cable television network to air on a broadcast network.

It was a bold experiment. NBC got some new programming for its summer schedule, better than airing reruns. And Court TV used the opportunity to promo both their network and the fact that *Forensic Files* airs on Court TV every night of the week.

One of the episodes chosen for NBC was the story of a young model hit by a car and killed in the California desert while posing for photographs. The investigation dealt with the question of whether it truly was an accident.

As we usually do, we try to match re-creations to the actual evidence. In this case, we used the pictures taken by the suspect of the model that day. The re-creation showed the model sitting in the car, legs up on the dashboard, as the photographer took pictures outside, through the windshield.

A Court TV executive took me aside and said, "Look Paul, NBC . . . this is the big time. They won't put up with some of the edgy stuff you try to sneak into our shows, so don't be surprised when they tell you to cut that scene from the show."

A few days later, I got an E-mail from the NBC censor after reviewing the episode. (I'm paraphrasing here)

> Dear Paul:
> Regarding the scene where the model poses for pictures with her legs on the dashboard. Please remove the Lexus logo. Thank you.

You can't make this stuff up.

NINE

Some of Our Favorite Cases ... and Some Anecdotes

In some cases we've shown on *Forensic Files*, the perpetrators might have gotten away with their crimes, had it not been for advances in forensic science.

There is no such thing as "the perfect crime."

But, criminals occasionally do stupid things.

One man in Florida packed himself into a crate then shipped himself into his own building, intending to set it on fire for the insurance money after the employees left. Inside the crate, he had some flammable liquid to get the fire started and a walkie-talkie so he could call an accomplice to pick him up afterward.

So, what happened? When he pressed the "on" button of the walkie-talkie, it produced a spark that ignited the flammable liquid. There was a huge explosion which threw him into the air, through the roof, out into the parking lot about 250 yards away. What did he do next? He dusted himself off, hailed a cab and went to the nearest hospital to tend to his burns.

He got away with it too. He later went to South America for plastic surgery but kept his eye on the U.S. newspapers. When he thought the coast was all clear, he came back to the U.S. to claim the insurance money, not realizing the police were waiting for him. The police didn't reveal much about their investigation to the newspaper for this very reason.

We've already mentioned the story of Richard Crafts—the airline pilot who killed his wife then put her body through a wood chipper he set up next to a river. He was pretty clever, but two things tripped him up. He rented the wood chipper during a snowstorm—and paid for the rental by putting it on his credit card.

One of our all-time favorites was a man on a business trip to St. Louis. He says he went out jogging one morning and when he returned to his hotel room, found his wife dead in the bathtub. Apparently, she had drawn a bath, stepped into the tub, lost her footing, fell, hit her head and drowned. Not one but two autopsies were conducted in two different states. In both instances, pathologists could find no evidence of foul play. If it was murder, the husband got away with it.

Did he stop there? Of course not.

The husband then sued the hotel for negligence because there was a towel ring in the tub along with his wife's body that came out of the wall. The husband alleged that his wife must have grabbed hold of it as she fell and it was unable to hold her weight.

Facing a sizable lawsuit, the hotel hired an engineering firm to figure out how a one-hundred pound woman could have pulled this towel ring out of the wall, since it was screwed into metal studs, as the building code required.

Scientists found evidence of torque in the metal—which

meant that the towel ring was twisted toward the bathroom door. In other words, whoever pulled the towel ring from the wall, did so standing *outside* the tub.

The husband was convicted of murder based on this scientific evidence.

He got greedy. Amazing.

Here's another bizarre example of how killers can't seem to keep their mouths shut.

In Florida, a woman was killed and her son seriously injured after drinking soda that had been laced with poison. Police got suspicious when they discovered the man next door was a chemist, who had several run-ins with the family over their dog which ran on his property unchained.

While under surveillance, the neighbor sent party invitations to all his friends in the local Mensa group. Mensa is for people with exceptionally high IQs. The party was a "murder mystery weekend" at a nearby hotel. Police send an undercover officer to attend. And the case the guests were asked to solve? You guessed it—a woman killed by poison.

With a search warrant, police found a sample of the poison that killed his next-door neighbor in the man's garage.

In the Darlie Routier case that we described earlier, in which she said an intruder allegedly broke into her home, killed her two children, then attacked her with a knife before getting away. Emergency room doctors noticed the knife wounds on her chest were superficial—and nowhere near her brand new breast implants.

A coincidence? Not even the hospital employees believed it.

A perpetrator in the Midwest wanted to make sure he didn't leave his fingerprints behind. So, he took off his shoes and put his socks over his hands before entering the house. Unfortunately, he left his footprints all over the crime scene.

Another one of our all-time favorites was the story of a man living in Long Island, New York who retired and moved to Florida. The man who bought the house in Long Island found a locked steel drum in the crawl space labeled, "WARNING— CHEMICALS INSIDE." He wheeled it to the curb but trash collectors refused to take it. So the homeowner opened the drum and found the decomposed body of a young woman. X-rays showed she had been pregnant.

Also in the drum was an address book so badly degraded that the names and phone numbers were no longer visible. A forensic document examiner using ultraviolet light deciphered one of the names and a telephone number, which by this time, was more than twenty years old.

Police called the number and were surprised to learn it was still in service. And, the woman listed in the address book still lived there. She was able to identify the woman in the steel drum as her best friend, an immigrant from El Salvador. She mysteriously disappeared while working in a factory owned by the man who previously lived in the Long Island home.

Why didn't he simply take the steel drum with him when he moved to Florida? We'll never know. He shot himself in the head before police could arrest him.

You'd think policemen would make good criminals. Not always.

The arson case involving Seattle cop, Matt Bachmeier, required the investigators to believe the unlikely story that Bachmeier just "happened" to remove all of his prized bowling trophies from his home just before the mysterious fire. Saving those bowling trophies was enough to land him behind bars.

There must be something about cops and suspicious fires.

Another cop in Green Bay Wisconsin also owned a home that was destroyed by fire. His estranged wife was living there alone and died in the fire. The medical examiner found evidence the woman was dead before the fire started. All of the doors were locked. The ex-husband had the only other known set of keys.

The cop's fiance was suspicious and she started taping their conversations. The cop admitted he went to see his wife on the day of the fire, contradicting the story he told to homicide investigators. Some cop.

Producing each *Forensic Files* episode is a complicated ordeal. For every case chosen, at least fifty are rejected. Once chosen, the stories are shot where they happened, which means some are shot in foreign countries. When the filming is done, there is approximately twenty-four hours of footage (1,440 minutes) which is edited down to just twenty-two minutes. The transcripts of the experts and family members who are interviewed total approximately 80,000 words. Since I read every word of every interview for every show, that's like reading a novel a week.

After the program is put together in rough-cut form, the re-creations are shot. This can be difficult because we need to match the actual crime scene. Sometimes we're able to find just the right location. If not, we build elaborate sets. Casting requires finding actors who look like the actual participants in the case, or coming as close as possible, which isn't always easy.

Editing any broadcast television show is a complicated affair. With hours of footage, hundreds of pages of interviews, crime scene photographs, forensic 3-D animation and the re-creations, there are plenty of creative and editorial options. Woody Allen's movie, *Annie Hall,* which won the Academy Award®, contained about three-hundred fifty edits in the ninety-minute film. A twenty-two-minute *Forensic Files* episode can have as many as eight-hundred edits or more.

217

The music is composed for each episode in Hollywood, the sound effects are added, it's mixed in Dolby surround sound back here in Pennsylvania, then the shows are duplicated, translated and shipped to Court TV and around the world. From start to finish, each episode takes approximately five months to complete—and there are as many as a dozen episodes in production at any given time.

For reasons we're still trying to figure out, we're never able to shoot the re-creations for the crimes in the same season in which they occurred. Crimes that happen in the winter inevitably end up on our schedule in the summer months, requiring snow machines, winter clothing for the actors, and production assistants to remove the leaves on trees you can see in the background!

And shooting crimes committed in the summer during the winter months necessitates having the actors use all sorts of tricks (like those ice cubes) to make sure you won't see their breath in the cold air.

If you're familiar with the series, you'll know that many of these cases involve fires, car wrecks, trains, buses, and trucks crashing into each another, plus people jumping from speeding cars, gunfire through windows and doors, pyrotechnics, miniature trains and cars, blood spatter in strategic locations, and many other challenges.

We often use trained animals when the forensic evidence calls for it: dogs, cats, pigeons, mice, rats, snakes, and even a trained squirrel. That squirrel was amazing. He did exactly what he was told and never ran away, even though we were shooting at night on a golf course! His trainer insisted he be allowed to take a short nap between takes. Perhaps he wanted to look good for his close-up!

When a re-creation requires rain, snow, fog, fire, or a windstorm, it's all done by some fine special-effects people. Safety is always an element in the production planning, but things don't always go perfectly. We were shooting the story of a woman who killed her husband then set fire to his hotel room to make it look like he fell asleep with a lit cigar. After shooting the preliminary scene with the live actors, we cleared the set and replaced the husband with a dressed mannequin for the fire sequence.

After the shooting was complete and the fire extinguished, the crew took their lunch break. I asked if it was safe to leave the set unattended. After all, there had just been a full blaze! Everyone assured me it was fine.

I wasn't convinced, so when everyone left, I picked up the burnt mannequin and carpet, stuffed it all into trash cans and hauled them outside before joining the crew for lunch. Not three minutes later, the trash cans were totally ablaze. The whole Medstar building would have gone up. We shoot fire scenes differently now, needless to say.

I occasionally direct some of the re-creations, which is always an adventure. Once, we were shooting a scene with a ventriloquist, who was hired to perform his nightclub routine, and we had all sorts of audio problems.

After we set the lights and got the camera into position, I walked off to the side of the set, put on my headset and sat in front of the monitor to watch the action. I could hear the ventriloquist fine, but when the dummy spoke, it was barely audible. When I told the ventriloquist the problem, he said "I'm throwing my voice as loud as I can and it works just fine in my nightclub act. I don't know why you're not hearing it."

"Well," I said, "try it again." I walked back out to the monitor, put on my headset, and the same thing happened. I couldn't hear the dummy.

So I asked the ventriloquist to do his bit one last time while I stood next to the soundman who was holding the boom microphone. I soon learned the cause of the problem. The

soundman was moving the microphone from the ventriloquist over to the dummy when it was his turn to speak.

The soundman insisted it was a joke, but I'm not so sure.
What amazed me was that the ventriloquist didn't notice.

You truly can't make these things up!

A Few Final Words

On October 3, 1995, like almost everyone else in the U.S., I anxiously awaited the verdict in the O.J. Simpson murder trial, wondering how the jurors would interpret the vast amounts of forensic evidence, knowing that most of them weren't experts in science.

Needless to say, I was surprised by the not-guilty verdict. We had already begun shooting the first *Forensic Files* episodes. At the time, I was researching a case about Timothy Spencer, the first man executed in the U.S. based on DNA evidence. Interestingly, there was more DNA evidence against O.J. Simpson than there was against Timothy Spencer.

The jury deliberated for less than four hours. Hearing the words "not guilty" reinforced the idea I had had all along for *Forensic Files,* and that was to explain forensic science to lay people: how it's collected, how it's tested, what it can tell you, and what it can't.

Science tries to explain the natural world in a rational way. Scientists put forth a hypothesis, then test that theory as rigorously as possible. If it withstands those tests, it's accepted. What I hope I'm doing with *Forensic Files* is explaining science in a way viewers can understand.

We are about to air our two-hundredth episode. Prosecutors and scientists tell us that jurors today are better-educated, more aware and sophisticated that they were five years ago, thanks in some measure to programs like *Forensic Files*. When we first started, we gave detailed descriptions of what tests like Luminol, mitochondrial DNA, and mass spectometry could do. Now, focus group participants say "We know what those are, Tell us something we don't know."

Forensic science continues to evolve in fascinating ways. Every day, scientists find new ways to uncover the truth about what really happened at a crime scene. New software programs, advances in microbiology, chemistry, and genetics provide ways to solve crimes far more convincingly that an eyewitness.

History will undoubtedly remember the twentieth century as one of outstanding scientific achievement. Most of that new science was used to solve crime.

As I write this, I am in the planning stages of at least a dozen new episodes, including one with the working title "The Alibi," which I call "the best episode I haven't yet produced." It's the story of a married woman and her lover who were found murdered. Her husband, a famous prosecutor in line for a judgeship, had an airtight alibi for the night of the murder. He was in another state at the time with numerous witnesses who confirmed that. An airtight alibi can often overcome, in the jury's collective mind, much circumstantial evidence. But forensic evidence is another matter . . .

I'm also thinking about the next *Forensic Files Casebook*. Per-

Peter Thomas, the narrator of *Forensic Files.* He's the man we call "The Franchise." He's a born storyteller and a class-act.

haps we'll include the anatomy of a show—a day-by-day account of how an episode of *Forensic Files* makes it to air, from beginning to end. Who knows? Maybe we'll explain how the "Alibi" episode was accomplished if we get it done in time. Or, just maybe, I'll finally be able to convince those network executives to approve the "too hot for air" episodes.

Stay tuned!

223

About the Authors

PAUL DOWLING created *Forensic Files,* and serves as executive producer/writer. He is founder and president of Medstar Television, which, since its inception in1982, has grown to become one of the largest producers of health and medical television programming in the U.S.

In addition to *Forensic Files*, Mr. Dowling has produced and written numerous television series, documentaries, and specials in the fields of forensic science, medicine, and health, among them *Medical Detectives*, "Your Health," on The Discovery Channel, and an HBO special hosted by Walter Cronkite.

Mr. Dowling holds bachelor's and master's degrees from The Juilliard School in New York City.

VINCE SHERRY has been a producer and writer for *Forensic Files* since 1998. He served in the same capacity for *Medical Detectives*, a CableACE nominee for best documentary series that appears nationally on The Learning Channel and internationally on the Discovery Channel.

From 1990–1995 he served as Tokyo-based Senior Producer/Writer for "Asia Now," a co-production between PBS and the Japan Broadcasting Corporation (NHK). This capped more than a decade working as a journalist and TV producer in Asia.

Mr. Sherry grew up in Emmaus, Pennsylvania, and holds a degree in radio, television, and film from Temple University.